EASY PIANO

PHIL COLLINS TS

ISBN 978-0-634-02036-0

HAL•LEONARD®
CORPORATION
7777 W. BLUEMOUND RD. P.O. BOX 13819 MILWAUKEE, WI 53213

Visit Hal Leonard Online at
www.halleonard.com

ANOTHER DAY IN PARADISE

Words and Music by
PHIL COLLINS

Medium Rock Ballad

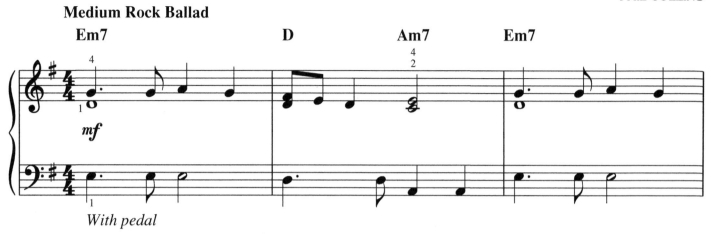

With pedal

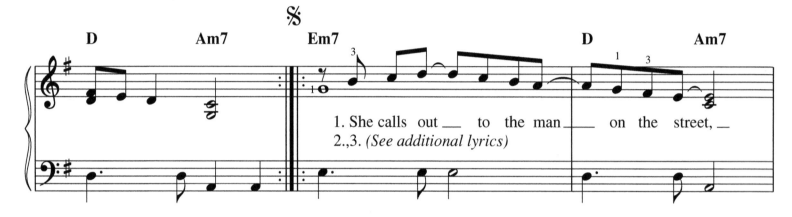

1. She calls out __ to the man __ on the street, __
2.,3. *(See additional lyrics)*

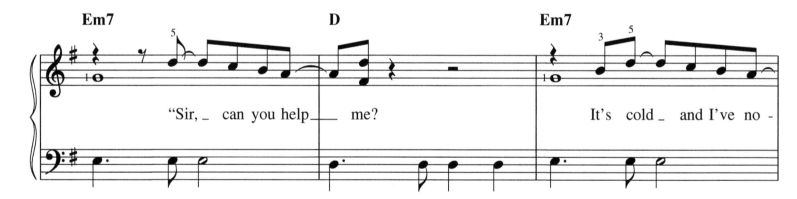

"Sir, __ can you help __ me? It's cold __ and I've no-

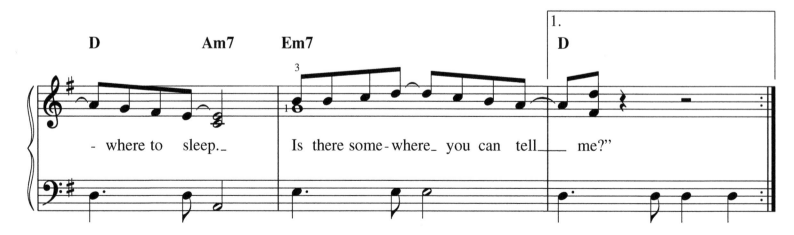

- where to sleep. __ Is there some-where __ you can tell __ me?"

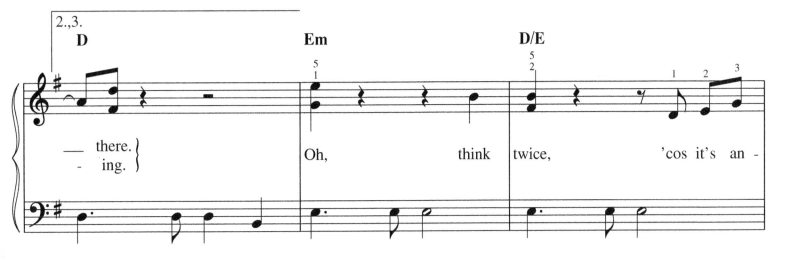

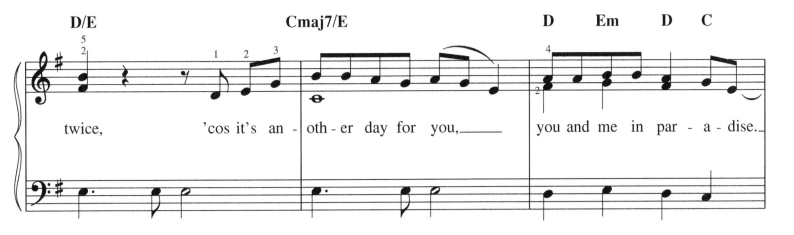

4

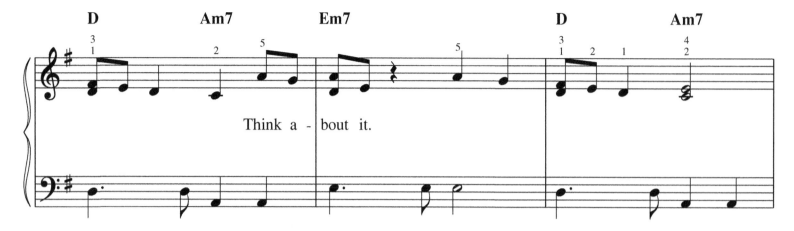

Think a - bout it.

To Coda ⊕

D.S. al Coda

CODA

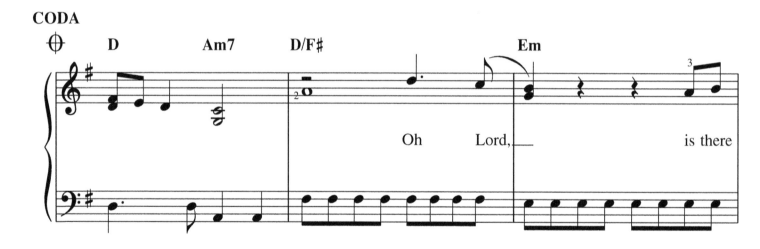

Oh   Lord,___   is there

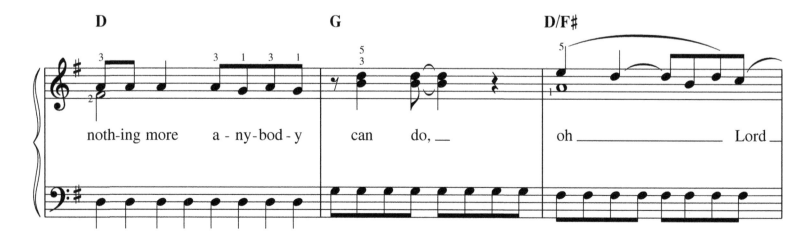

noth-ing more   a - ny-bod - y   can   do, ___   oh _____ Lord ___

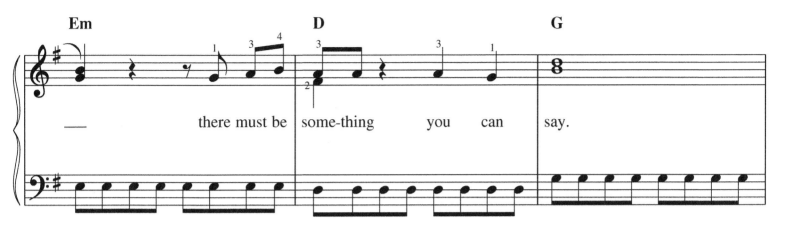

there must be some-thing you can say.

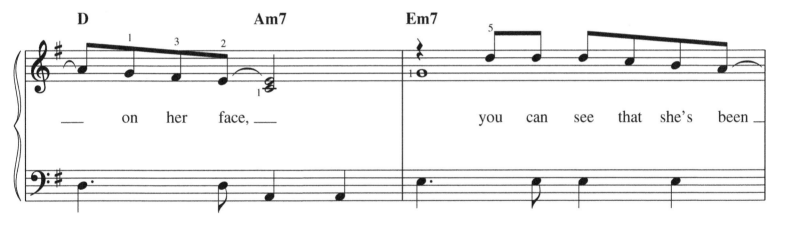

You can tell ___ from the lines ___

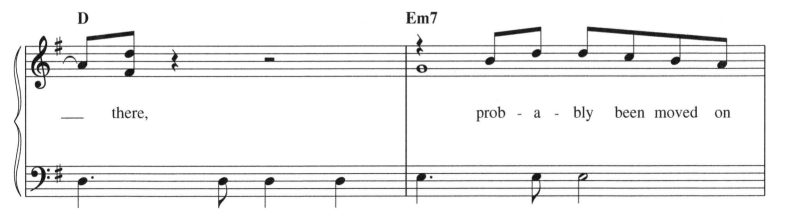

on her face, ___ you can see that she's been

___ there, prob - a - bly been moved on

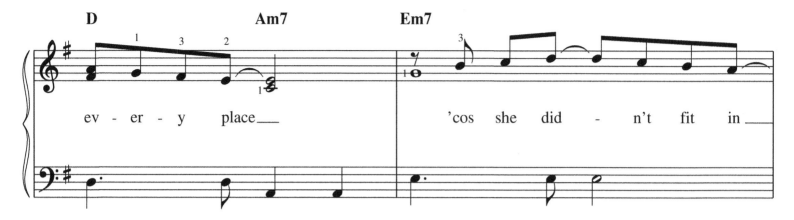

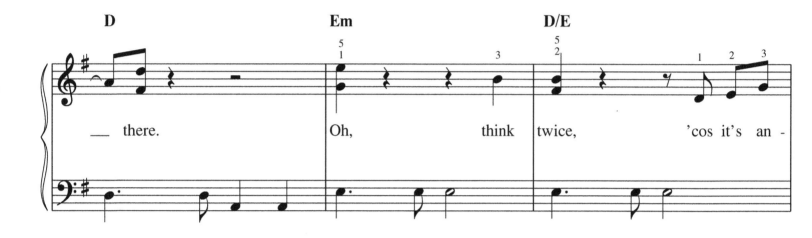

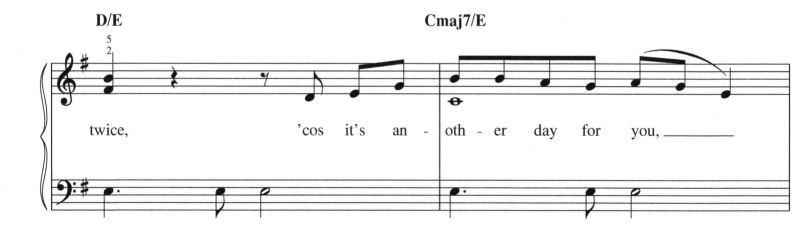

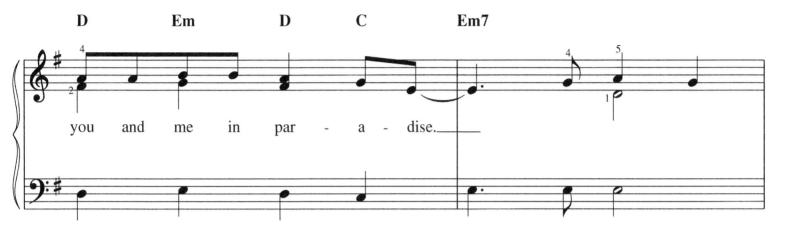

you and me in par - a - dise.

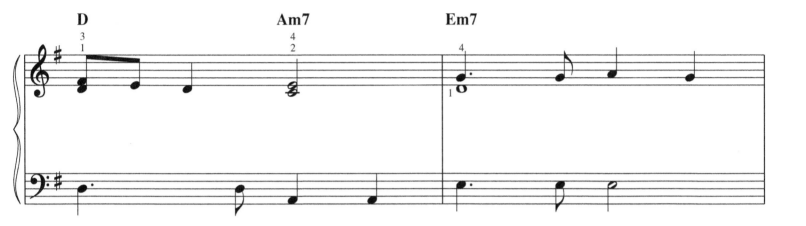

Think a - bout it.

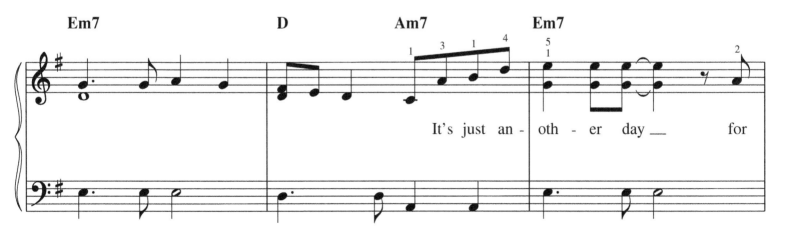

It's just an - oth - er day ___ for

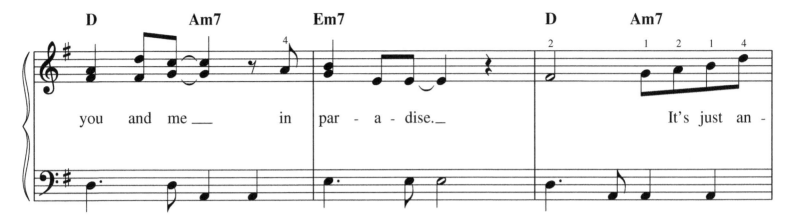

you and me ___ in par - a - dise.___ It's just an-

oth - er day ___ for you and me ___ in par - a - dise. ___

Additional Lyrics

2. He walks on, doesn't look back,
   He pretends he can't hear her,
   Starts to whistle as he crosses the street,
   Seems embarrassed to be there.

3. She calls out to the man on the street,
   He can see she's been crying,
   She's got blisters on the soles of her feet,
   She can't walk, but she's trying.

TRUE COLORS

Words and Music by BILLY STEINBERG
and TOM KELLY

Moderately slow

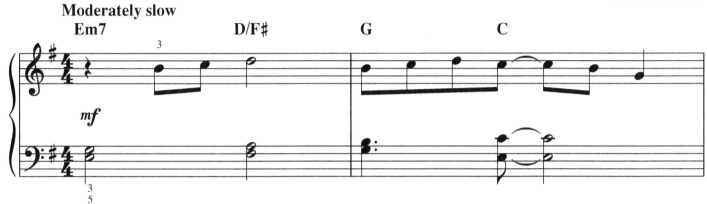

You with the

sad   eyes
smile _____

don't   be   dis - cour - aged   to   a -
don't   be   un - hap - py   can't   re -

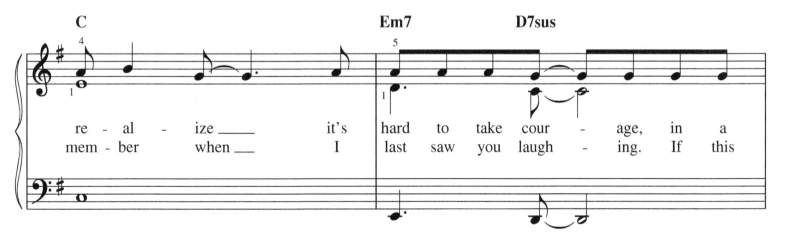

re - al - ize _____   it's
mem - ber   when ___   I

hard   to   take   cour - age,   in   a
last   saw   you   laugh - ing.   If   this

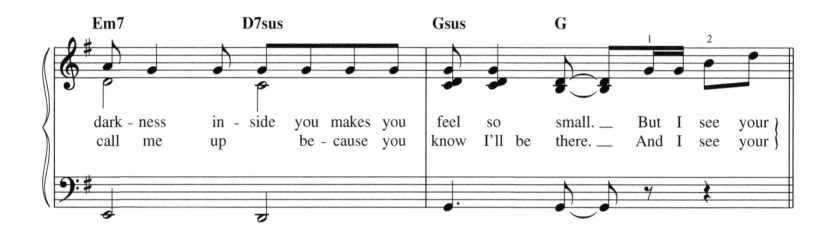

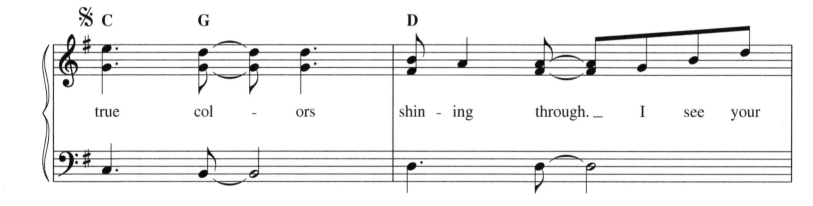

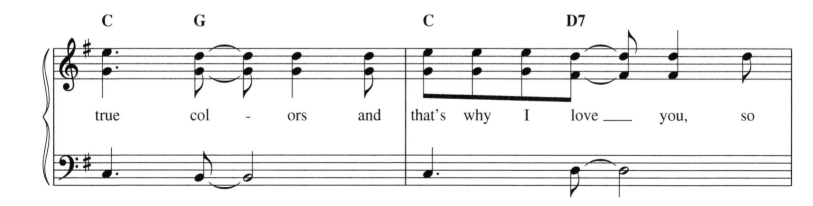

don't be a - fraid ____ to let them show, ____ your

To Coda

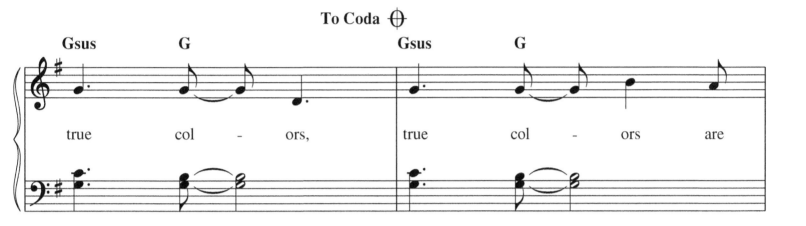

true col - ors, true col - ors are

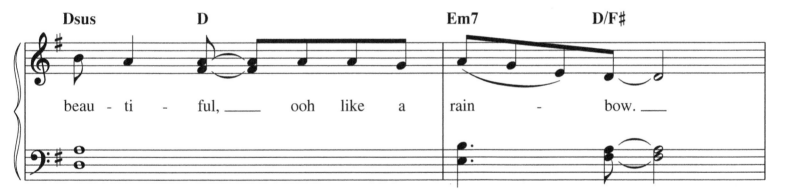

beau - ti - ful, ____ ooh like a rain - bow. ____

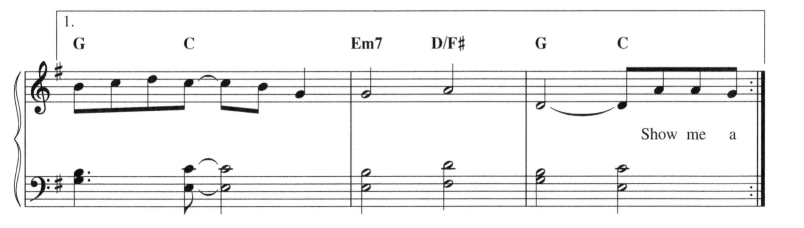

Show me a

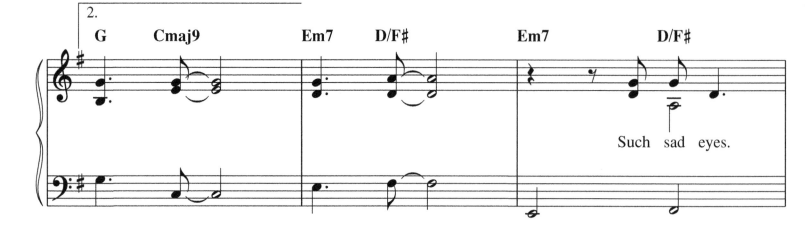

Such sad eyes.

Take cour - age now, __ re - al - ise _____ when

this world makes you cra - zy and you've tak - en all you ___ can bear,

just call me up be - cause you know I'll be there. __ And I see your

CODA

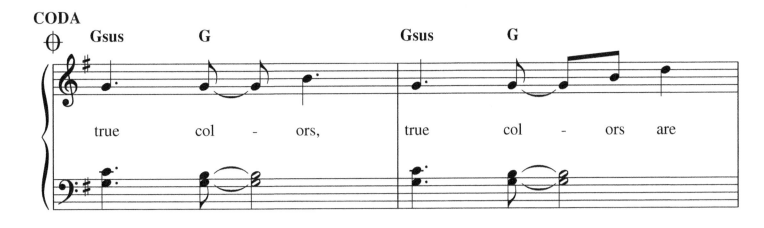

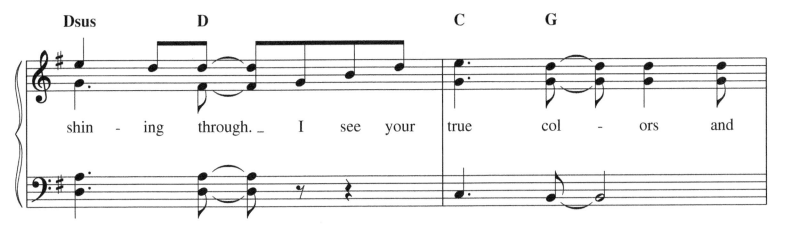

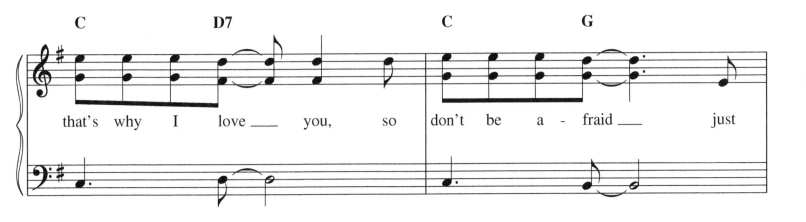

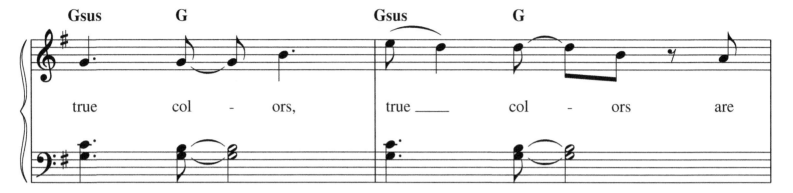

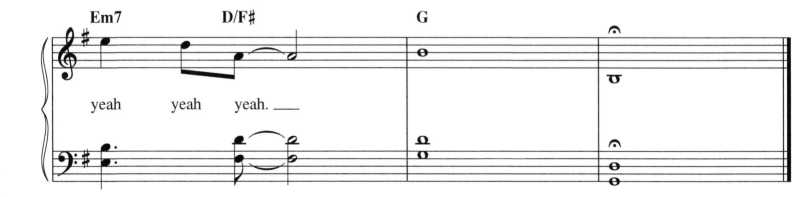

EASY LOVER

Words and Music by PHIL COLLINS,
PHILLIP BAILEY and NATHAN EAST

Medium tempo

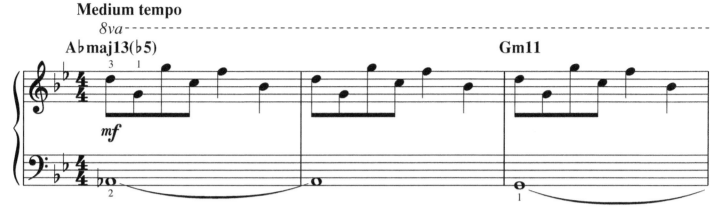

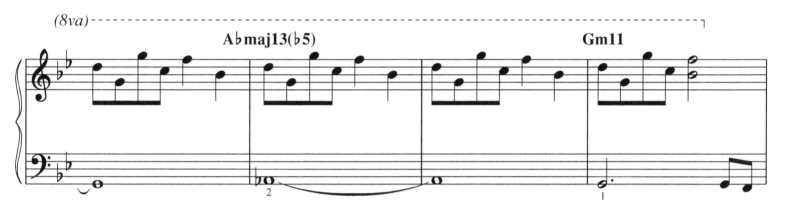

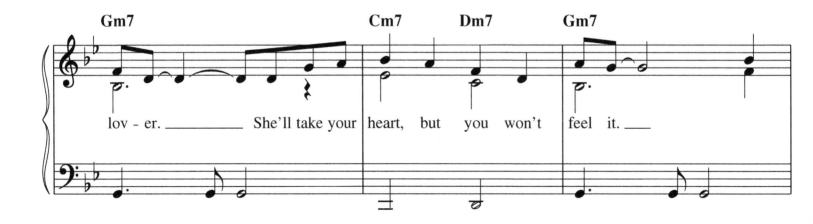

She's like no oth - er, _____ and I'm just try'ng to make you

see.

She's the kind of girl you dream of,
You're the one that wants to hold her,

dream of keep-ing hold of.
hold her and con-trol her.

Bet-ter for - get it. __
Bet-ter for - get it. __

You'll _ nev - er get it. __
You'll _ nev - er get it. __

She will
'Cause she'll

play a- round and leave you,
say that there's no oth - er

leave you and de-ceive you.
till she finds an - oth - er.

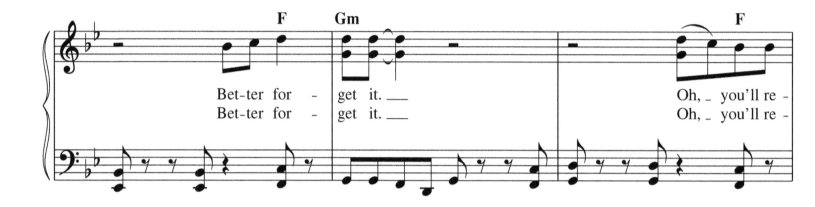

Bet-ter for - get it. __
Bet-ter for - get it. __

Oh, _ you'll re -
Oh, _ you'll re -

gret it. __
gret it. __

No, you'll nev-er change her, so leave her, leave her.
And don't try to change her. Just leave her, leave her.

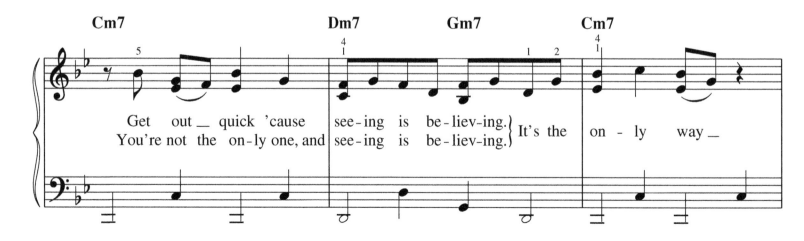

Get out _ quick 'cause see-ing is be - liev-ing.
You're not the on-ly one, and see-ing is be-liev-ing.

It's the on - ly way _

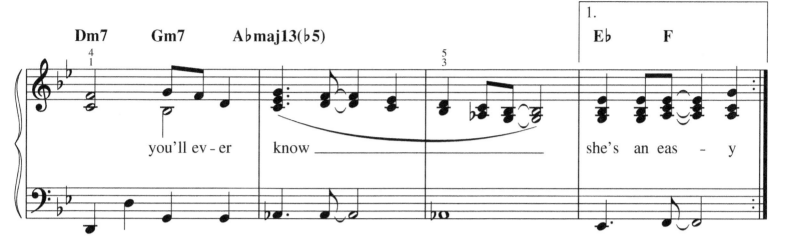

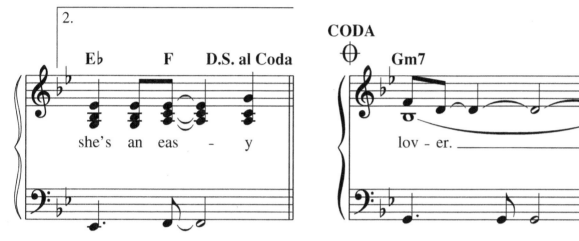

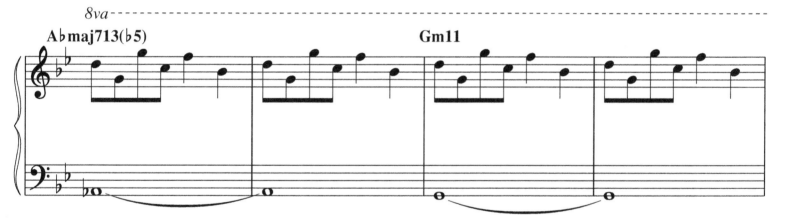

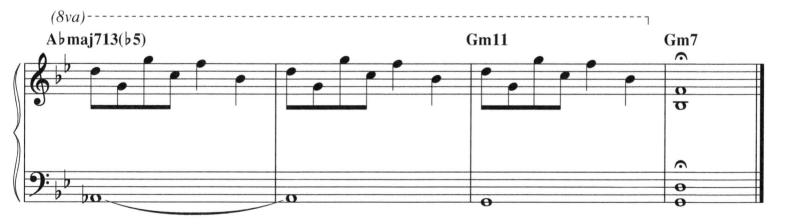

YOU CAN'T HURRY LOVE

Words and Music by EDWARD HOLLAND,
LAMONT DOZIER and BRIAN HOLLAND

Medium Rock

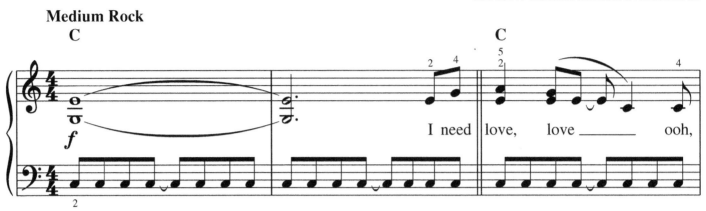

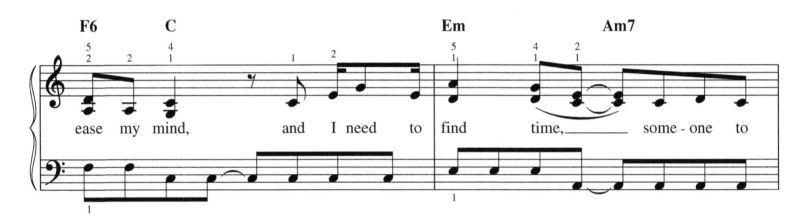

just have to wait, _ just trust on a good _ time, no mat-ter how long it takes."

How man-y heart - aches must I stand be-fore I find the love to let me

I can't bear _ to live my life a - lone. I grow im - pa - tient for a love to

live a-gain? Right now the on - ly thing that keeps me hang-in' on, when I

call my own. But when I feel that I, I can't go on, well, these

feel my strength, ooh, is al - most gone, } I re-mem - ber Ma-ma said, "You

pre - cious words keep me hang - ing on,

To Coda

can't hur - ry love, ___ no, you'll just have to wait." ___ She said,

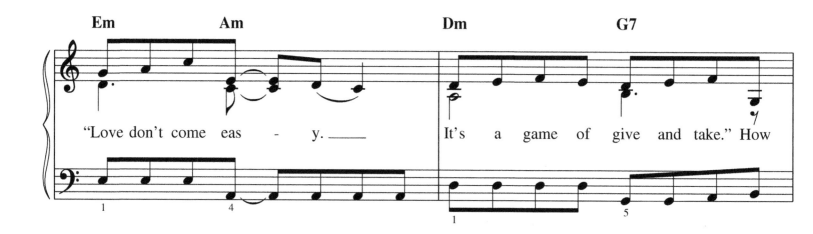

"Love don't come eas - y. ___ It's a game of give and take." How

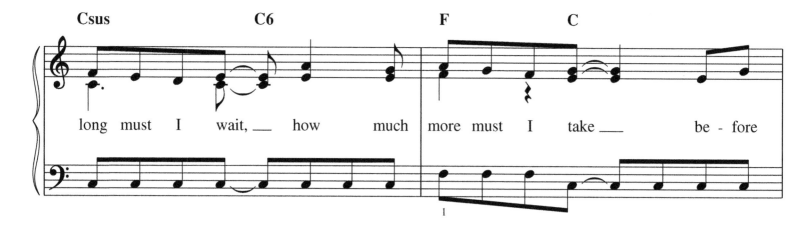

long must I wait, ___ how much more must I take ___ be - fore

D.S. al Coda

lone - li - ness ___ will cause my heart, heart to break? No

CODA

"Love don't come eas - y. ___ Well, it's a game of give and take. You

can't hur - ry love, ___ no you'll just have to wait, ___ just

trust on a good ___ time, no mat - ter how long it takes, now

break!" Now love, love ___ don't come

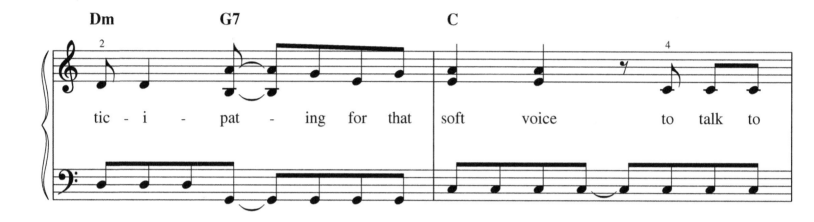

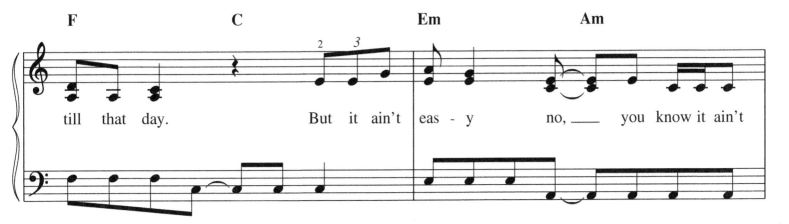

TWO HEARTS

Words and Music by PHIL COLLINS
and LAMONT DOZIER

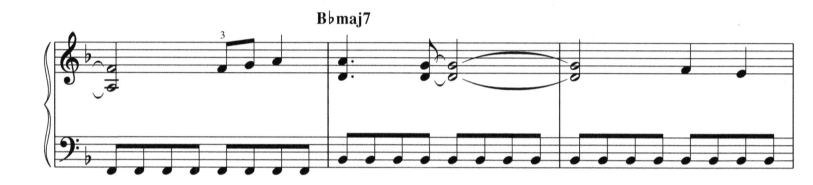

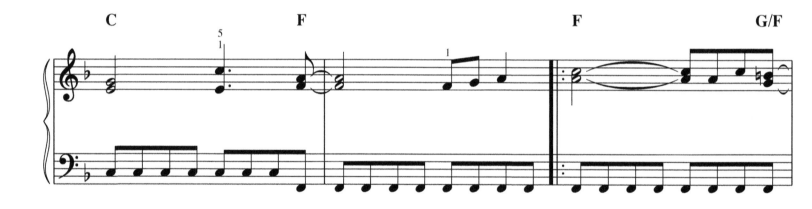

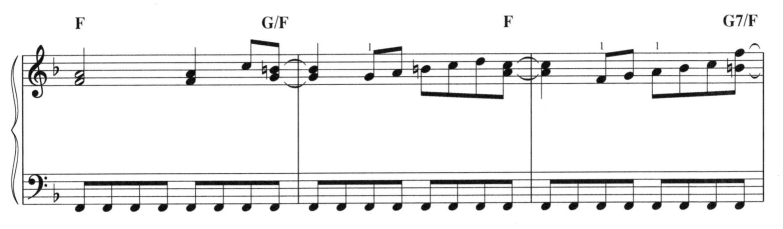

1. There was no rea - son to be - lieve
2. *(See additional lyrics)*

___ she'll al - ways be there._ But if you don't put

faith in what you be - lieve in, it's get-ting no - where._

'Cause it helps you nev-er give up,___ don't look down,

___ just look up.___ 'Cause she's al-ways there_ be-hind

Chorus

___ you,_ just_ to re-mind_ you. Two hearts ___ / Two hearts ___

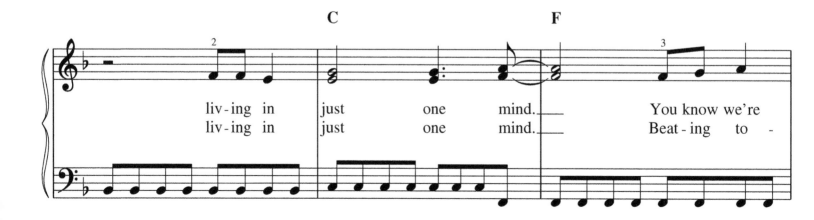

liv-ing in just one mind.___ You know we're
liv-ing in just one mind.___ Beat-ing to -

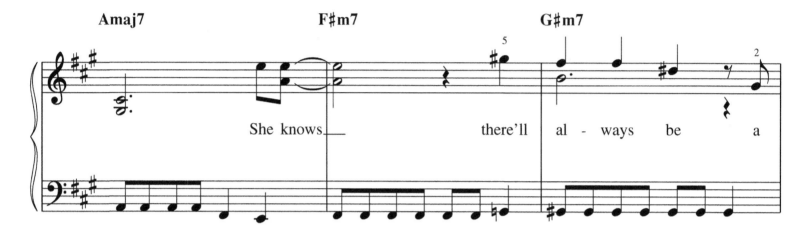

She knows___ there'll al - ways be a

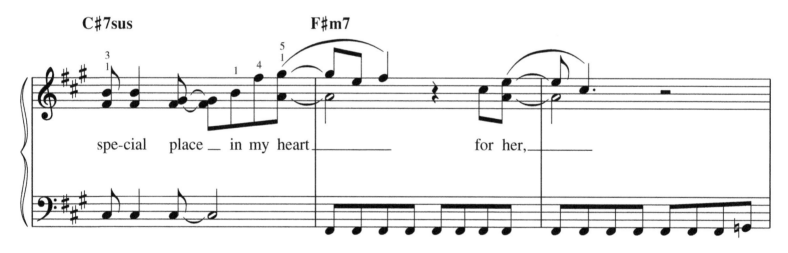

spe-cial place __ in my heart_____ for her,___

she knows,__ she knows,__ she knows.__ Yeah,__ she knows__

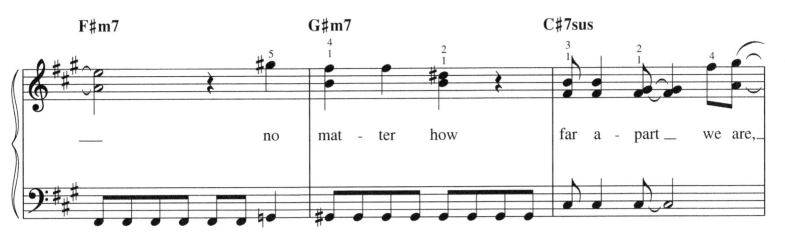

no mat - ter how far a - part _ we are,

_ she knows _ I'm al-ways right

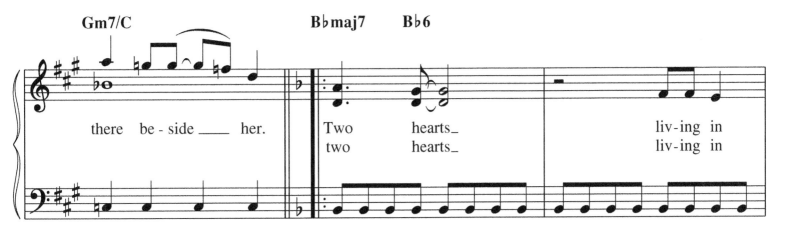

there be - side _ her. Two hearts _ liv-ing in
two hearts _ liv-ing in

just one mind, _ beat - ing to - geth - er _
just one mind, _ to - geth - er for- ev - er _

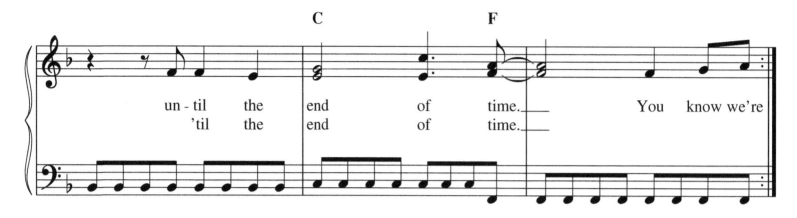

Additional Lyrics

2. Well, there's no easy way to, to understand it.
   There's so much of my life in her
   And it's like I planned it.
   And it teaches you to never let go,
   There's so much love you'll never know.
   She can reach you no matter how far,
   Wherever you are.
   Chorus

I WISH IT WOULD RAIN DOWN

Words and Music by
PHIL COLLINS

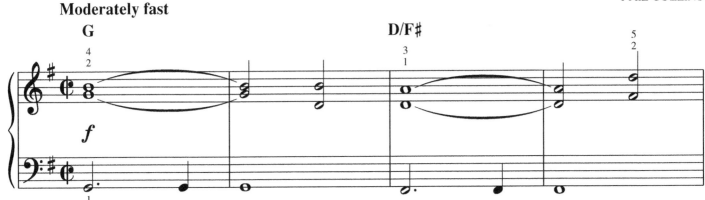

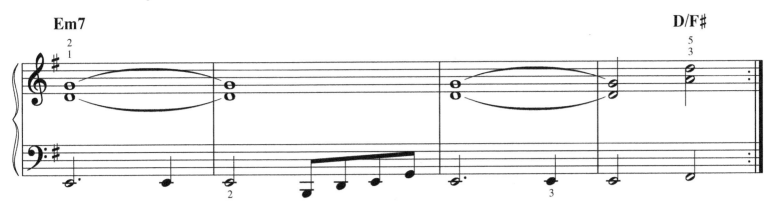

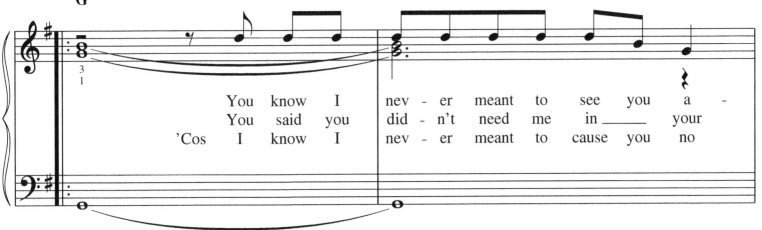

You know I never meant to see you a-
You said you didn't need me in _____ your
'Cos I know I never meant to cause you no

gain, and I only passed by as a friend, _____
life, oh I guess you _____ were right, _____
pain, and I re-a-lise I let you down, _____

all this
ooh I
but I

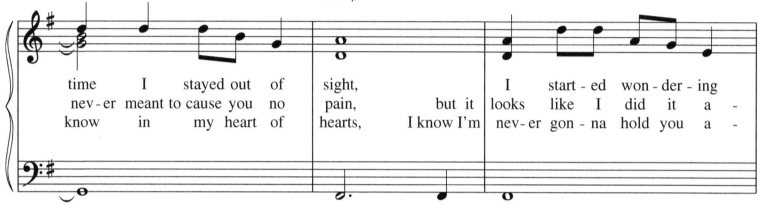

time I stayed out of sight, I start-ed won-der-ing
nev-er meant to cause you no pain, but it looks like I did it a-
know in my heart of hearts, I know I'm nev-er gon-na hold you a-

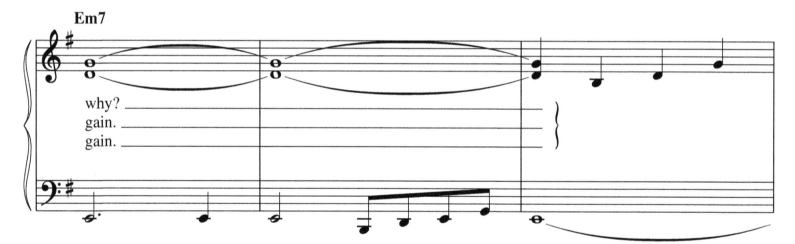

why? _____
gain. _____
gain. _____

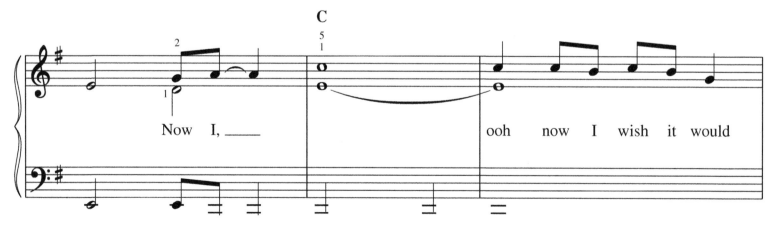

Now I, _____ ooh now I wish it would

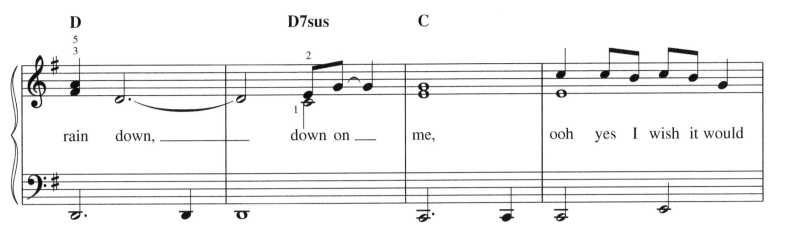

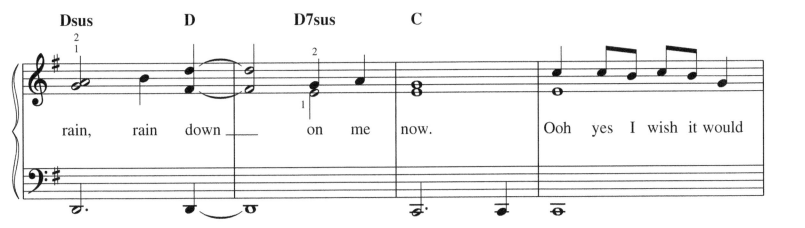

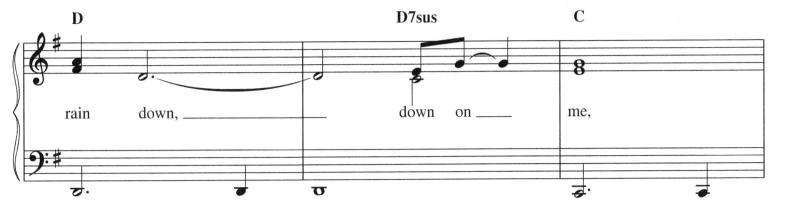

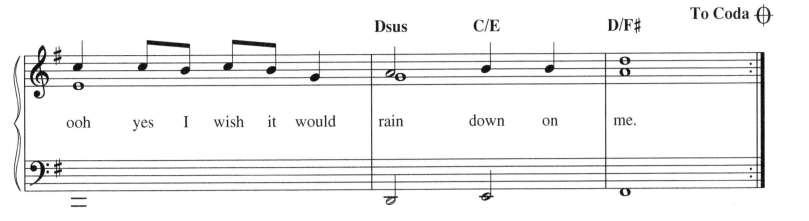

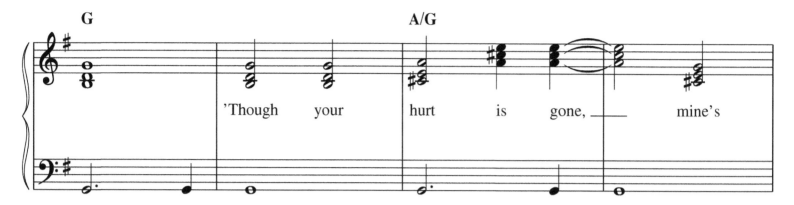

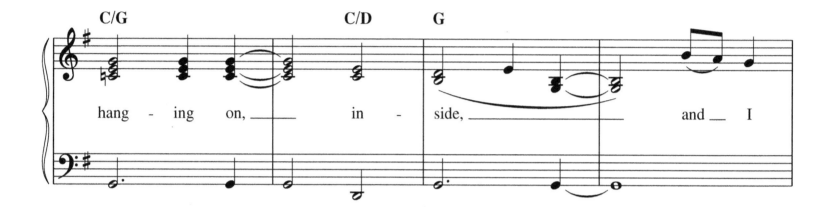

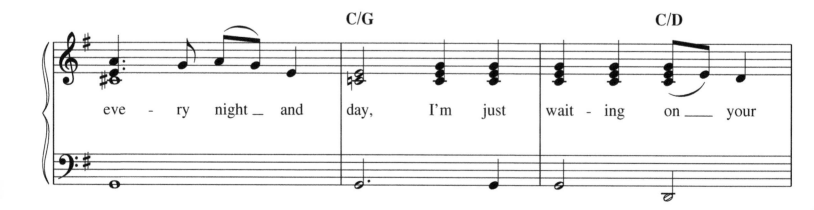

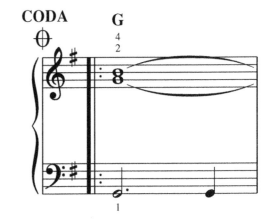

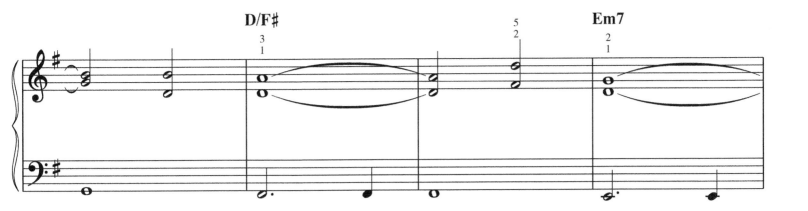

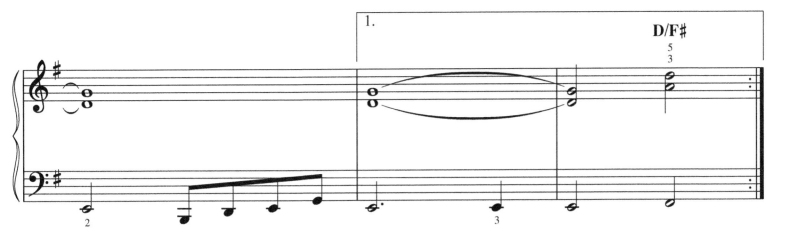

Just let it rain. _____

AGAINST ALL ODDS
(Take a Look at Me Now)

Words and Music by
PHIL COLLINS

Slow Rock

With pedal

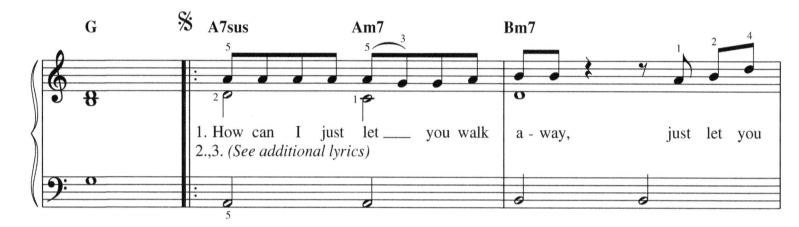

1. How can I just let ___ you walk a - way, just let you
2.,3. *(See additional lyrics)*

leave with - out ___ a trace? When I stand here tak - ing

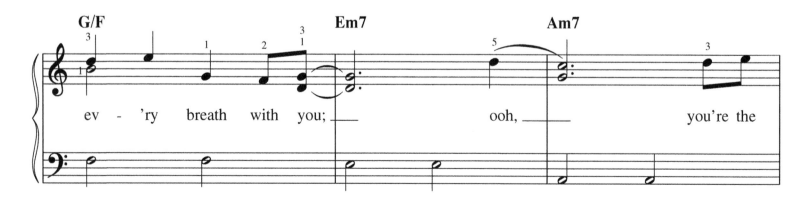

ev - 'ry breath with you; ___ ooh, ___ you're the

on - ly one who real - ly knew me ___ at all. ___

So take a look at me now,

well, there's just an emp - ty space. ___

And there's noth - ing left ___ here ___ to re - mind ___ me, ___ just the mem-

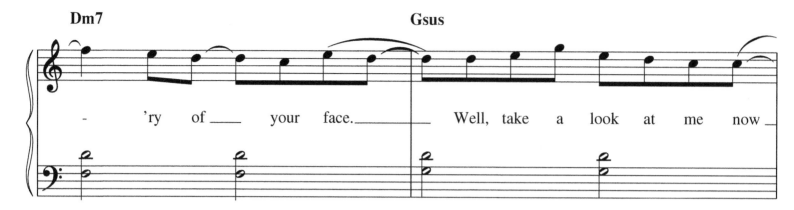

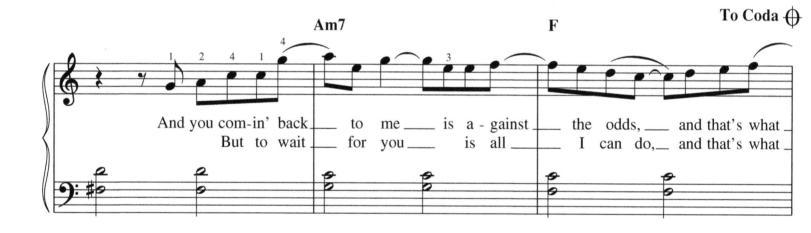

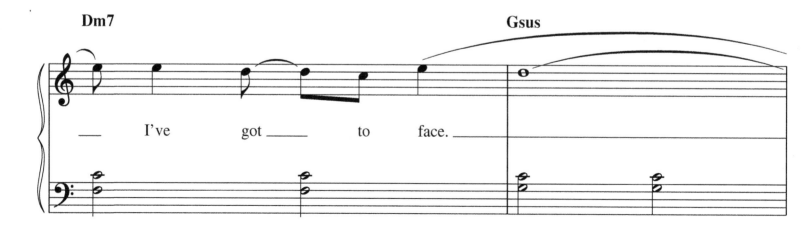

D.S. al Coda
(take 2nd ending)

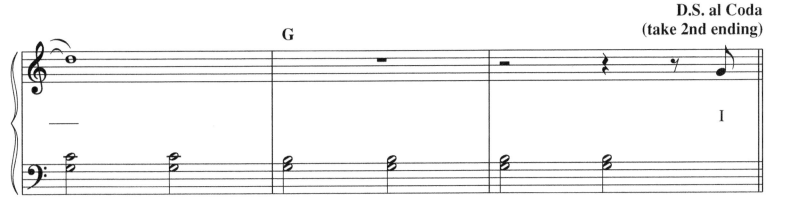

CODA

I've got to face. Take a good look at me now.

'Cause I'll still be stand-ing here. And you com-in' back

to me is a-gainst all odds, it's the chance I've got to take.

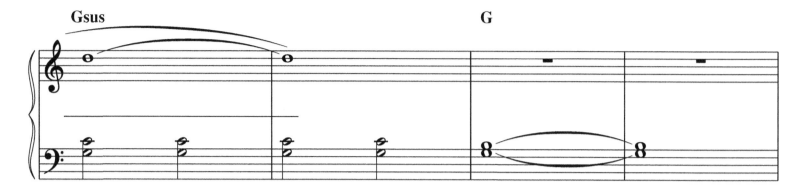

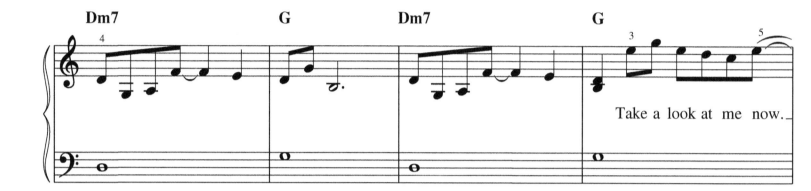

Take a look at me now.

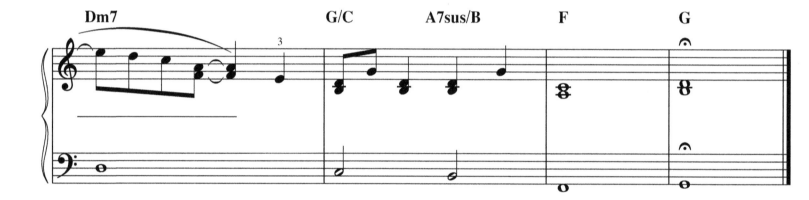

Additional Lyrics

2. How can you just walk away from me,
   When all I can do is watch you leave?
   'Cause we shared the laughter and the pain,
   We even shared the tears.
   You're the only one who really knew me at all.
   Chorus

3. I wish I could just make you turn around,
   Turn around and see me cryin',
   There's so much I need to say to you,
   So many reasons why.
   You're the only one who really knew me at all.
   Chorus

SOMETHING HAPPENED ON
THE WAY TO HEAVEN

Words and Music by PHIL COLLINS
and DARYL STUERMER

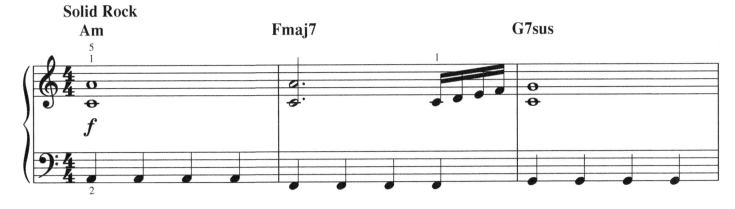

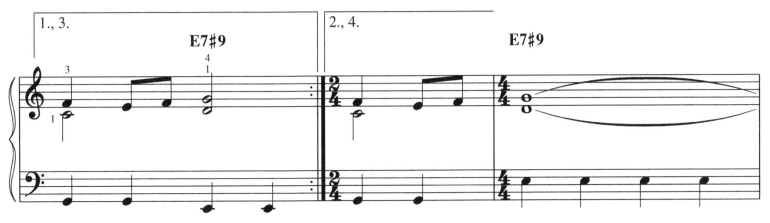

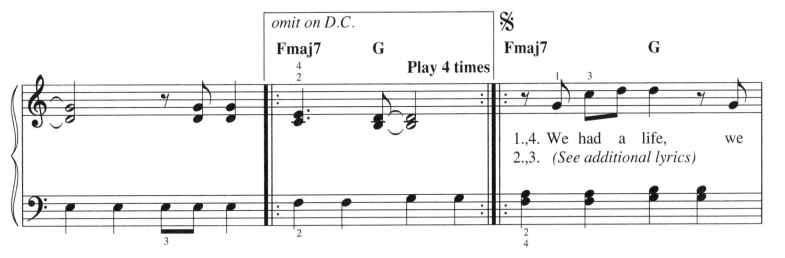

1.,4. We had a life, we
2.,3. (See additional lyrics)

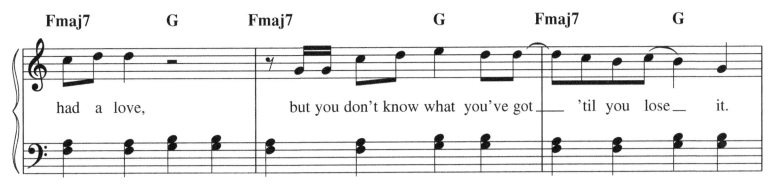

had a love, but you don't know what you've got ___ 'til you lose ___ it.

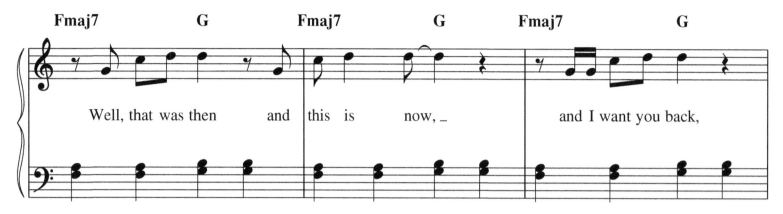

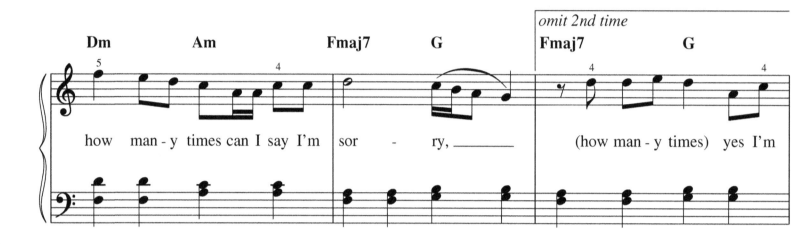

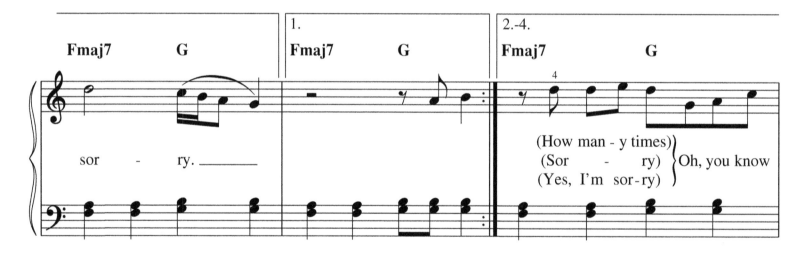

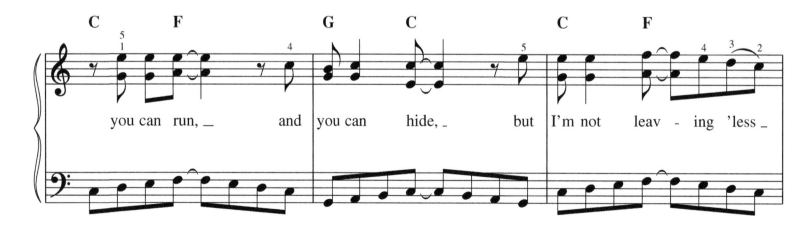

you come with me, we've had our prob-lems but I'm on your side,

you're all I need, please be-lieve in me.

Oh yeah.

please be-lieve me. You can run, and you can hide. but

I'm not leav - ing 'til __ it's all o - ver, we've had our prob-lems but I'm

To Coda ⊕

on your side, __ you're all I need, __ let me show __ you.

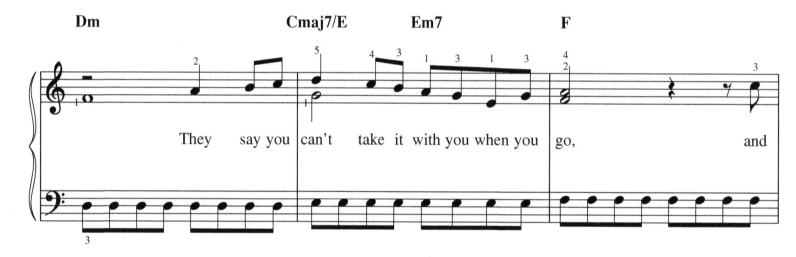

They say you can't take it with you when you go, and

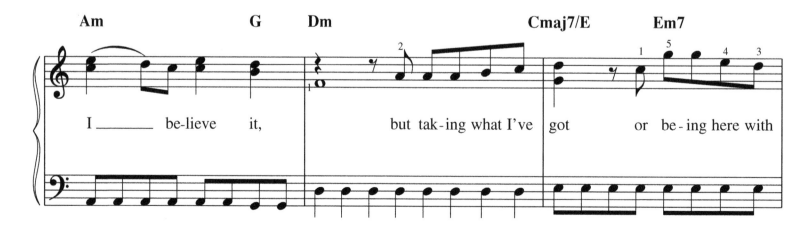

I _____ be-lieve it, but tak-ing what I've got or be - ing here with

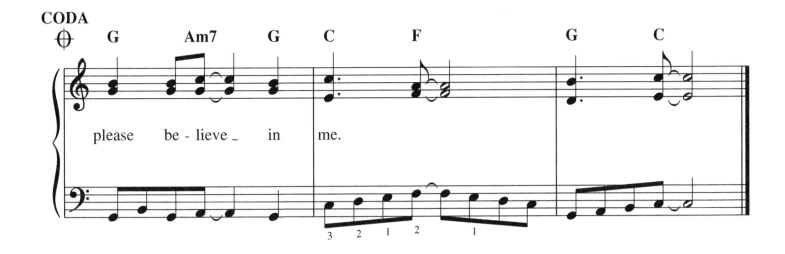

Additional Lyrics

2. How can something so good, go so bad,
   How can something so right, go so wrong,
   I don't know, I don't have all the answers,
   But I want you back,
   How many times can I say I'm sorry.
   (How many times.)

3. I only wanted you as someone to love,
   But something happened on the way to heaven,
   It got a hold of me, and wouldn't let go,
   And I want you back,
   How many times can I say I'm sorry.
   (How many times) yes, I'm sorry. (Sorry.)

SEPARATE LIVES
Love Theme from WHITE NIGHTS

Words and Music by
STEPHEN BISHOP

mp You called me from the room in your ho - tel

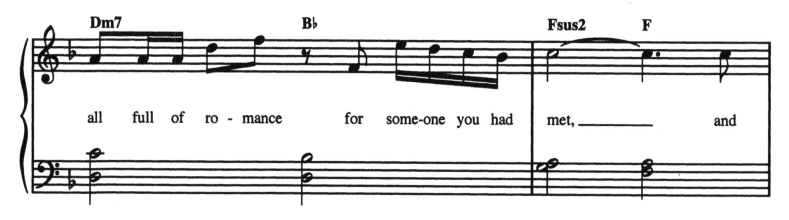

all full of ro - mance for some-one you had met, _____ and

tell - ing me how sor - ry you were leav-ing so soon, _____ and that you

miss me some-times _ when you're a - lone in your room. Do I feel lone - ly too?

Slowly, with expression

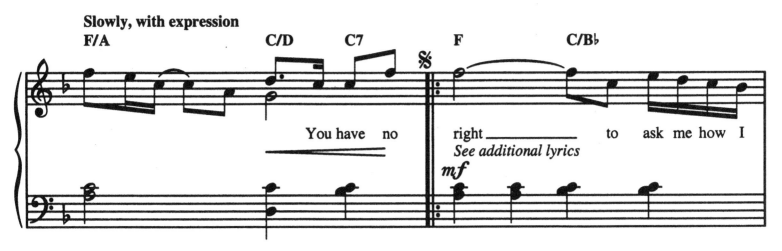

You have no right _____ to ask me how I

See additional lyrics

feel. _____ You have no right _____ to speak to me so

kind. _____ I can't go on hold - ing on _____ to

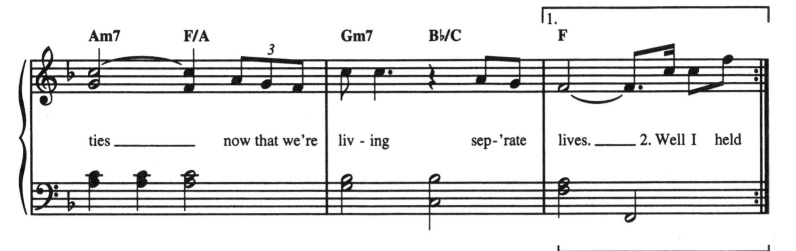

ties _____ now that we're liv - ing sep - 'rate lives. _____ 2. Well I held

50

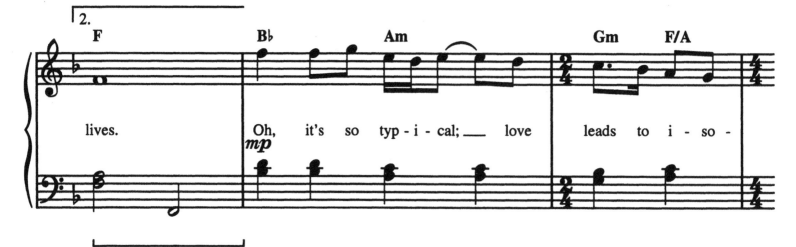

lives. Oh, it's so typ - i - cal; ___ love leads to i - so -

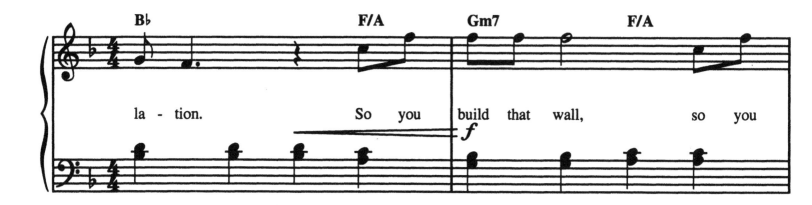

la - tion. So you build that wall, so you

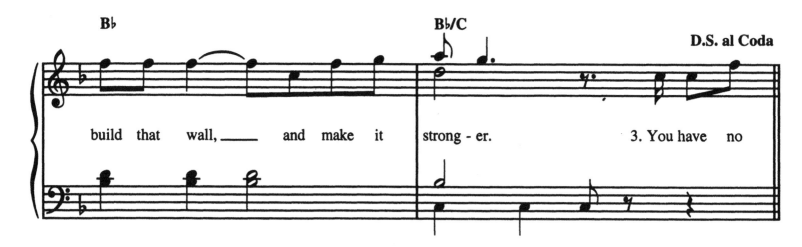

build that wall, ___ and make it strong - er. 3. You have no

D.S. al Coda

CODA

might find my - self look - ing in ___ your eyes. But for

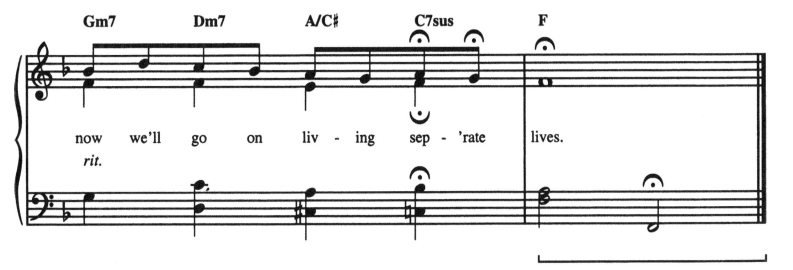

Additional Lyrics

Well, I held on to let you go.
And if you lost your love for me,
You never let it show.
There was no way to compromise.
So now we're living separate lives.

You have no right to ask me how I feel
You have no right to speak to me so kind.
Someday I might find myself looking in your eyes.
But for now, we'll go on living separate live.
Yes, for now we'll go on living separate lives.

BOTH SIDES OF THE STORY

Words and Music by
PHIL COLLINS

Moderately fast Rock

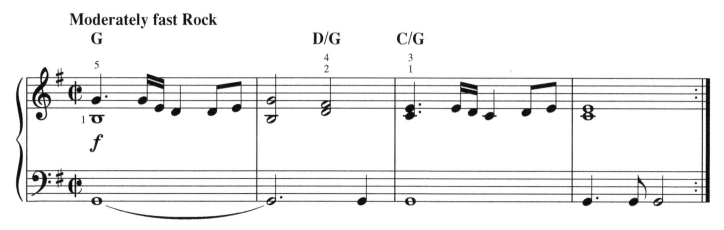

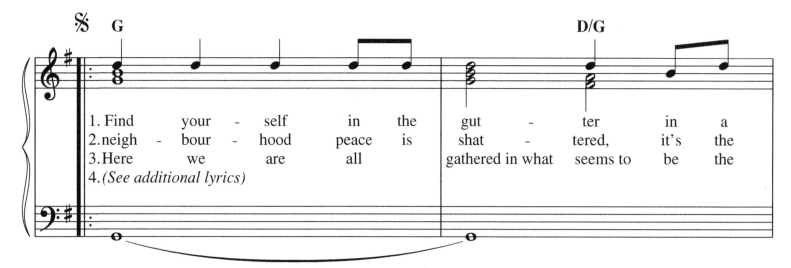

1. Find your - self in the gut - ter in a
2. neigh - bour - hood in peace is shat - tered, it's the
3. Here we are all gathered in what seems to be the
4. *(See additional lyrics)*

lone - ly part ____ of town, where
mid - dle of ____ the night, young
cen - tre of ____ the storm,

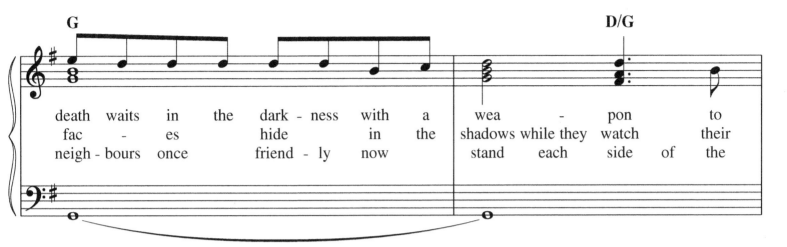

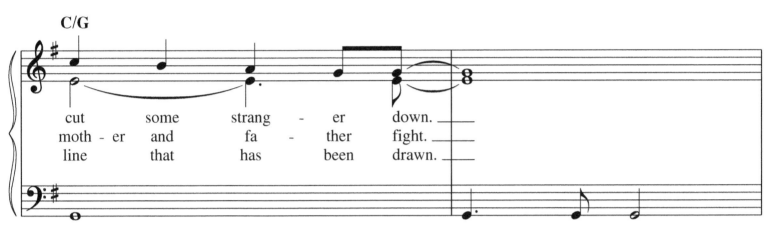

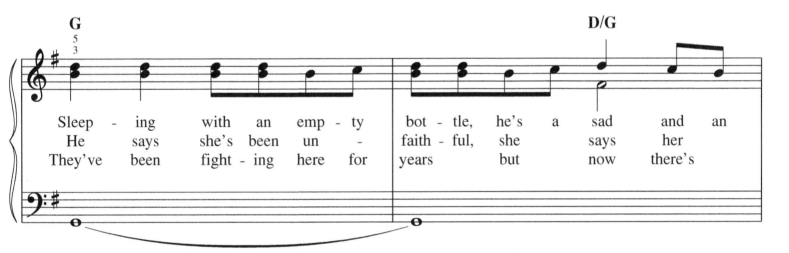

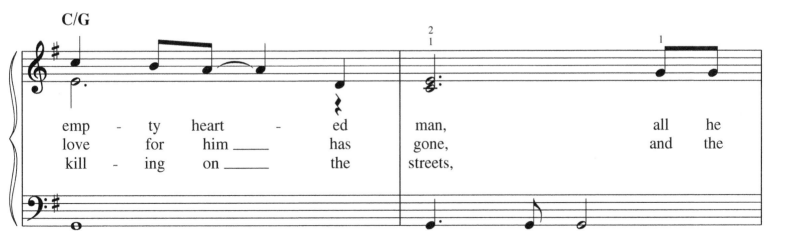

G

needs   is   a   job   and   a   lit - tle   re - spect, so   he   can
broth - er   shrugs   to   his   sis - ter   and   says, "Looks   like   it's
while   small   cof - fins   are   lined   up   sad - ly,   now   u -

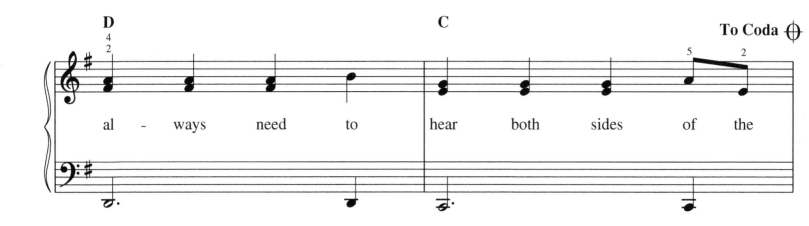

C/G

get   out   while   he   can.
just   us   from   now   on".
nit -   ed   in   de - feat.

We

D   **C**   **To Coda**

al - ways   need   to   hear   both   sides   of   the

1.

G   **D/G**   **C/G**

sto - ry,

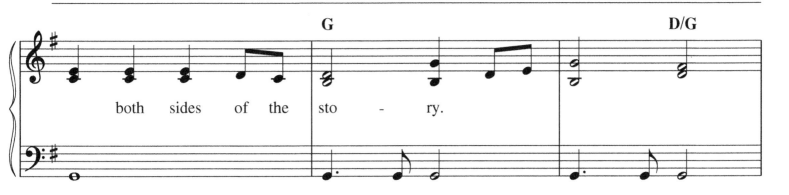

both sides of the sto - ry.

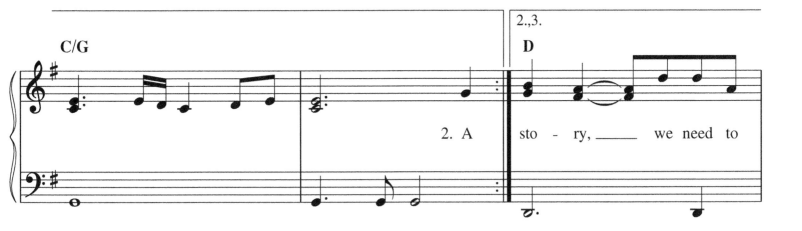

2. A sto - ry, _____ we need to

hear both sides of the sto - ry.

And the lights are all on, the world is watch - ing now. _____

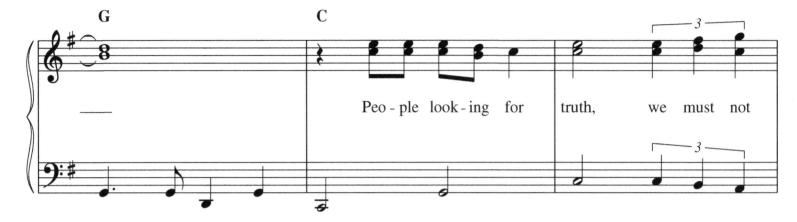

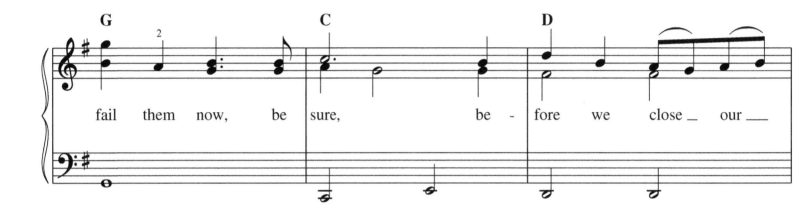

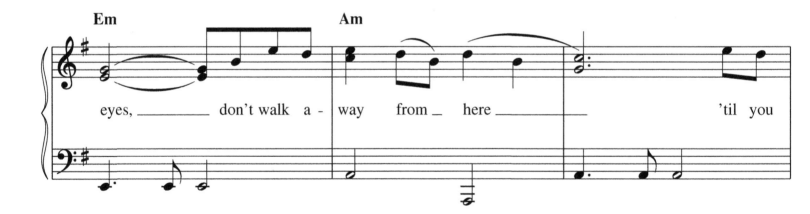

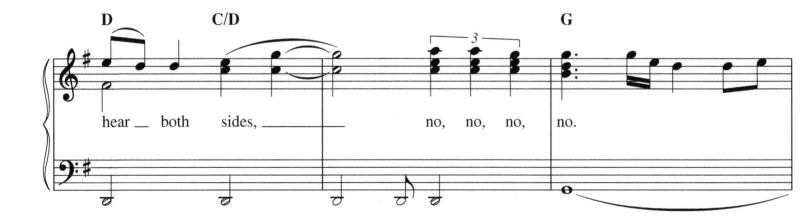

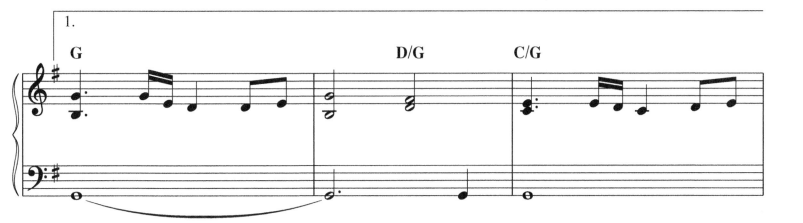

58

CODA

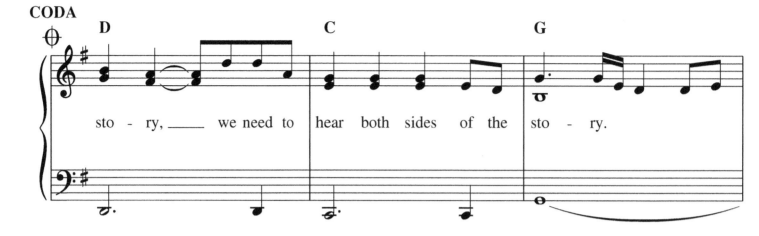

sto - ry, _____ we need to | hear both sides of the | sto - ry.

Additional Lyrics

4. White man turns the corner, himself within a different world
   Ghetto kid grabs his shoulder, throws him up against the wall
   He says, "Would you respect me if I didn't have this gun

ONE MORE NIGHT

Words and Music by
PHIL COLLINS

Slow Rock Ballad

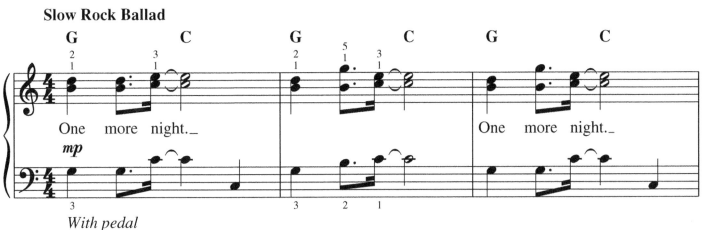

One more night.

mp

With pedal

One more night.

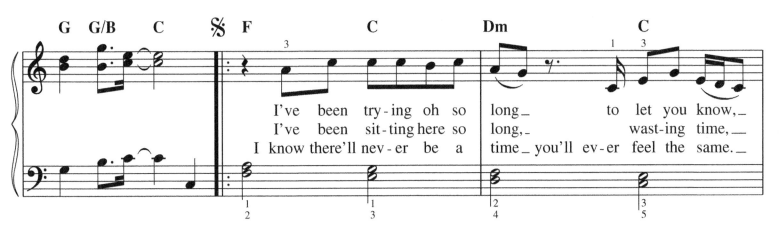

I've been try-ing oh so long_ to let you know,_
I've been sit-ting here so long,_ wast-ing time,_
I know there'll nev-er be a time_ you'll ev-er feel the same. _

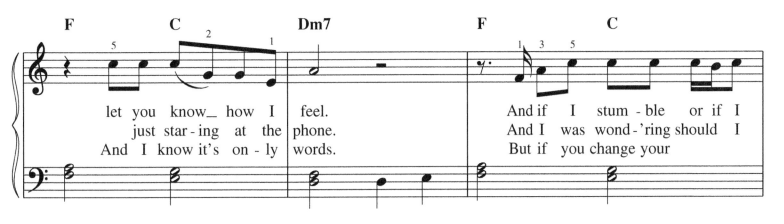

let you know_ how I feel.
just star-ing at the phone.
And I know it's on-ly words.

And if I stum-ble or if I
And I was wond-'ring should I
But if you change your

fall, ___ just help me back _____
call you, then I thought ___
mind, __ you know that I'll be here,

so I can make you
may-be you're not a -
and may-be we both can

To Coda ⊕

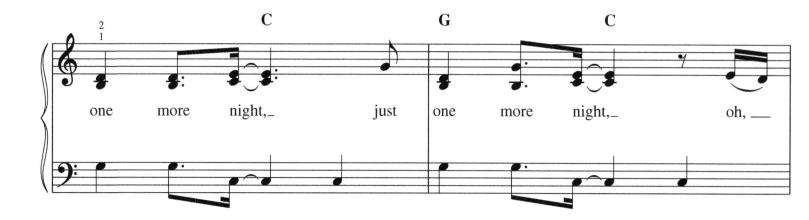

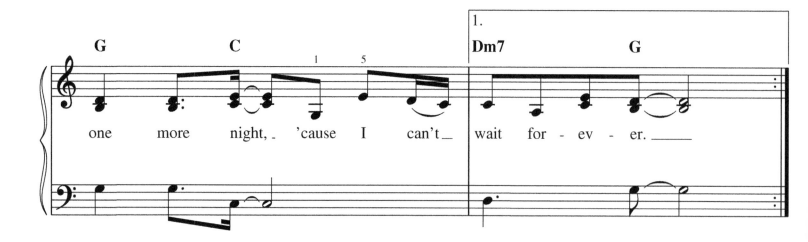

2.

wait for - ev - er.___ Give me one__ more night.__ Give me just one more night,__

one more night_ 'cause I ____ can't wait for - ev - er.___ Like a riv - er to the

sea, I will al - ways be with you. And if you sail a - way, I will fol - low you.__

_____ Give me one more night.__ Give me just one more night,__ oh,__

Dm7   **G**   **D.S. al Coda**

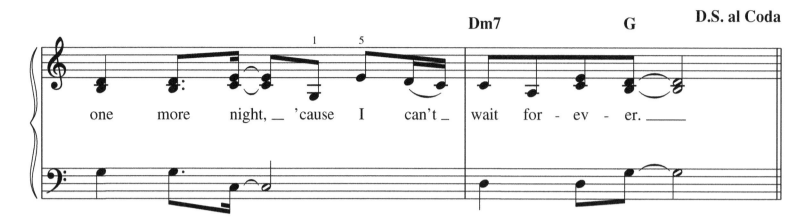

one more night, __ 'cause I can't _ wait for - ev - er. ____

CODA   **Dm7**   **G**   **C**

learn. _____ Give me just a   one ___ more night. _ Give me just a

G   **G/B**   **C**   **G**   **C**

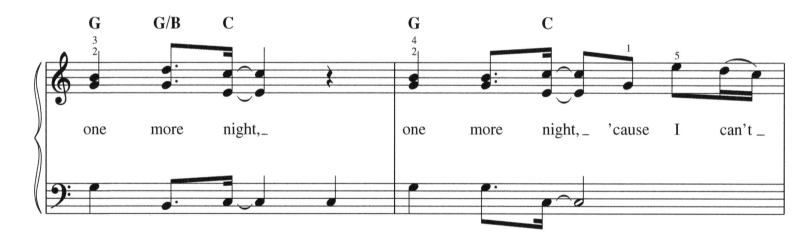

one more night, _   one more night, _ 'cause I can't _

1.
Dm7   **G**

wait for - ev - er. ___ Give me just a

2.
Dm7   **G**   **Cmaj9**

wait for - ev - er. ___

SUSSUDIO

Words and Music by
PHIL COLLINS

Up-tempo Rock

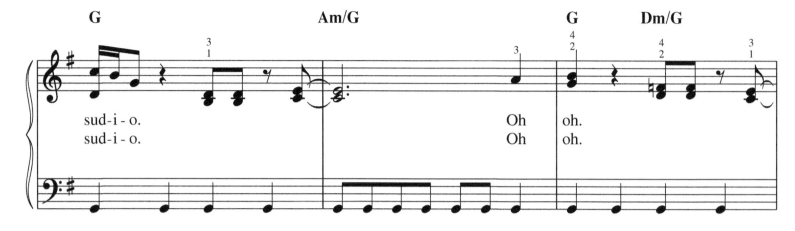

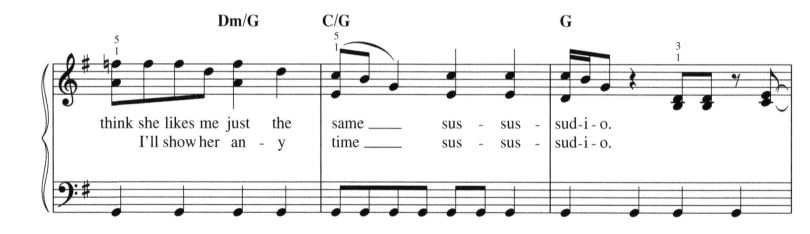

Oh, if she called me I'd be there, I'd come
Ah, I've got to have her, have her now, I've got to get

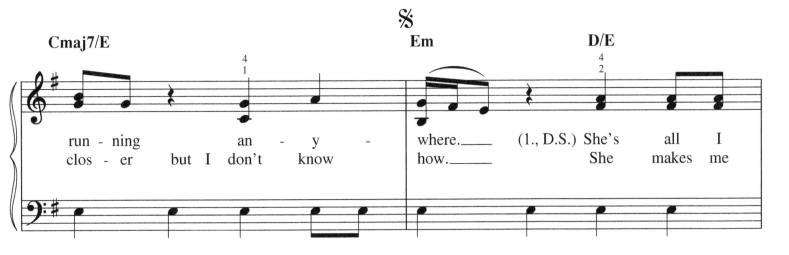

run - ning an - y - where. (1., D.S.) She's all I
clos - er but I don't know how. She makes me

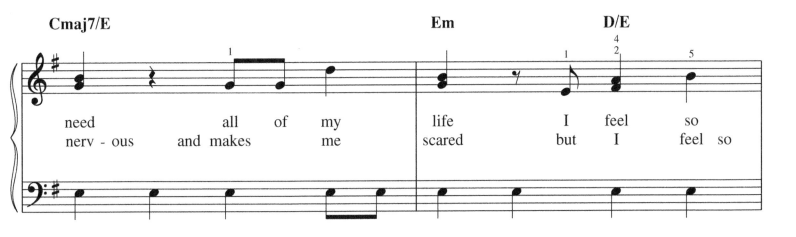

need all of my life I feel so
nerv - ous and makes me scared but I feel so

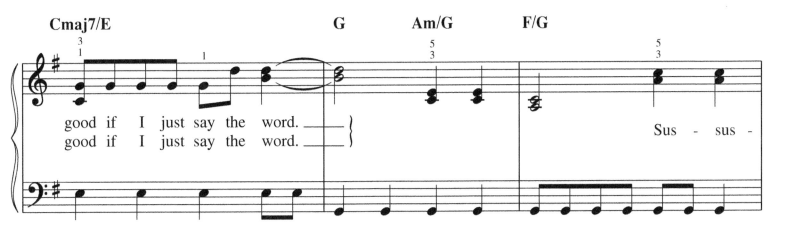

good if I just say the word.
good if I just say the word.
Sus - sus -

sud-i - o   just say the word   oh

To Coda ⊕ | 1.

sus - sus - sud-i - o._____

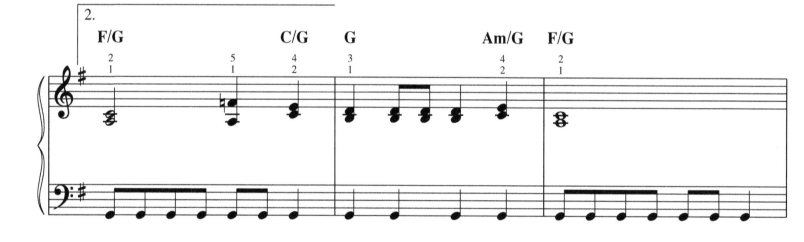

2.

67

D.S. al Coda

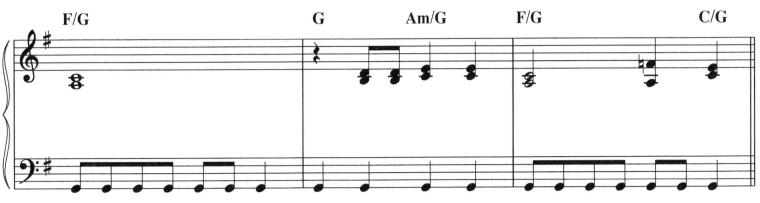

DANCE INTO THE LIGHT

Words and Music by
PHIL COLLINS

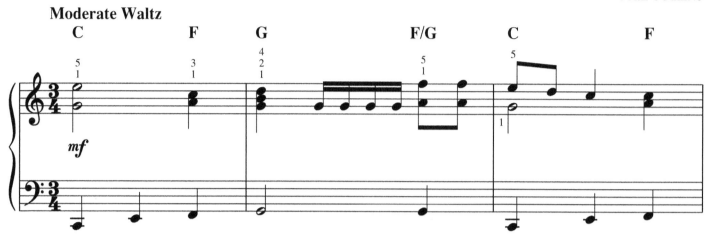

It's there in the eyes of the
There'll be no more hid - ing in the

chil - dren, in the
shad - ows of fear, there'll be

fac - es smil - ing in the win -
no more chains to hold

dows.
you.

You can come on out, come on
The fu - ture is yours, you

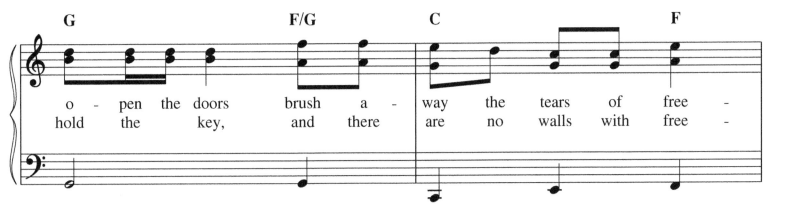

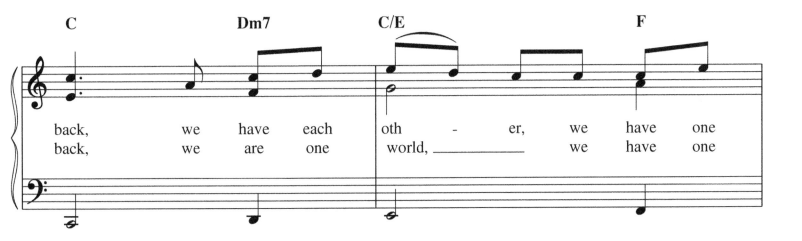

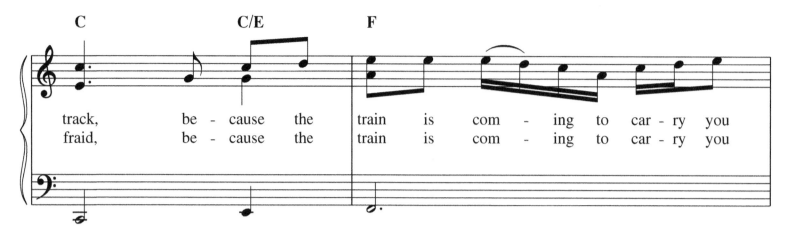

track, be - cause the train is com - ing to car - ry you
fraid, be - cause the train is com - ing to car - ry you

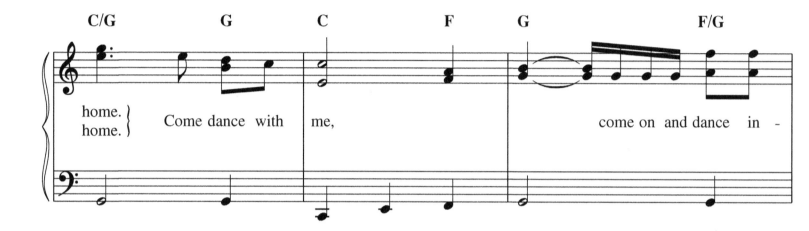

home. ⎫
home. ⎭ Come dance with me, come on and dance in -

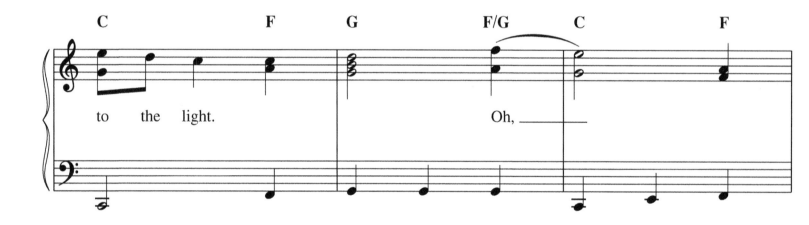

to the light. Oh, ___

ev - 'ry-bod - y dance in - to the light.

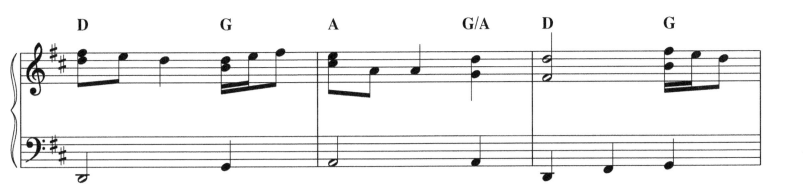

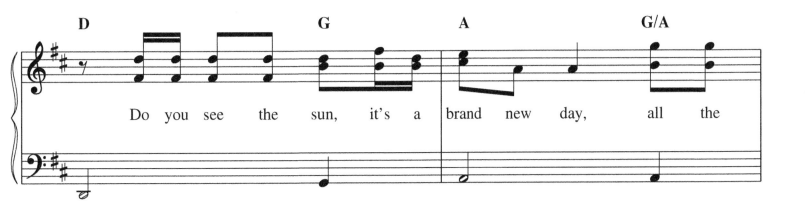

Do you see the sun, it's a brand new day, all the

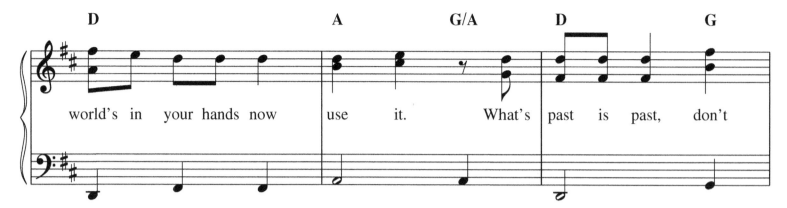

world's in your hands now use it. What's past is past, don't

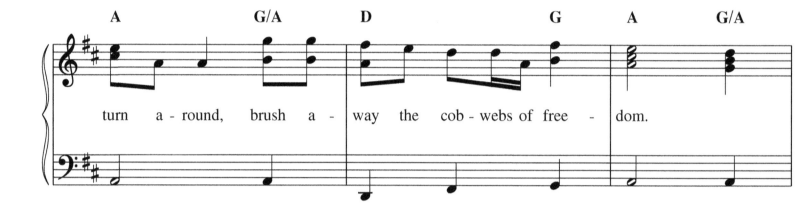

turn a - round, brush a - way the cob - webs of free - dom.

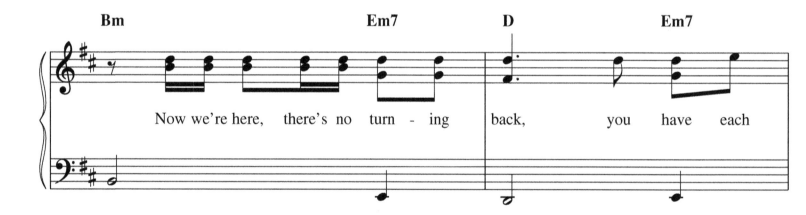

Now we're here, there's no turn - ing back, you have each

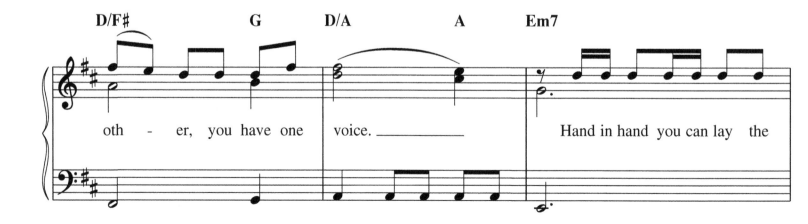

oth - er, you have one voice. _____ Hand in hand you can lay the

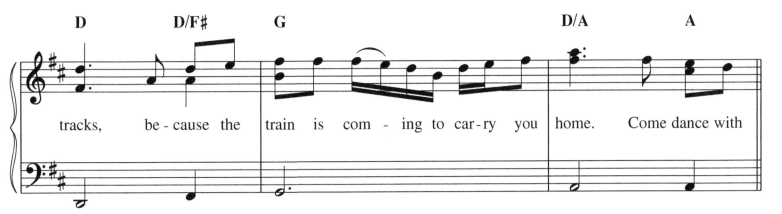

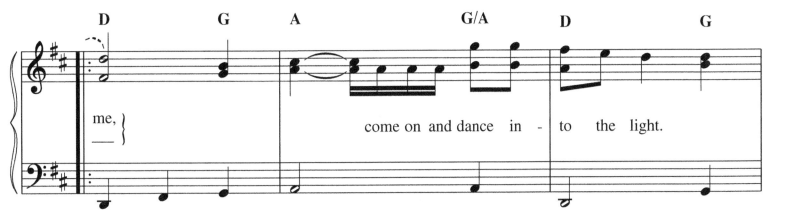

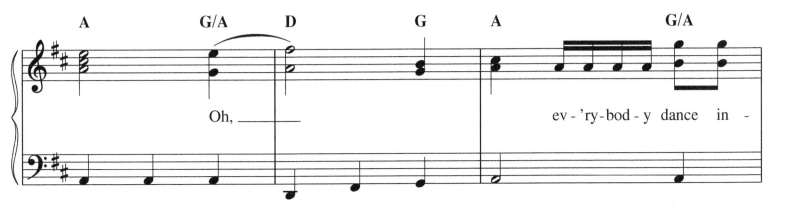

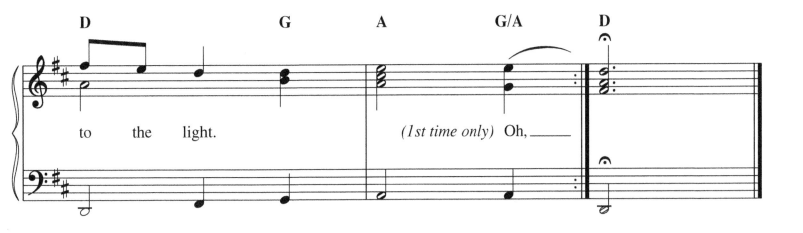

A GROOVY KIND OF LOVE

Words and Music by TONI WINE
and CAROLE BAYER SAGER

Slowly

With pedal

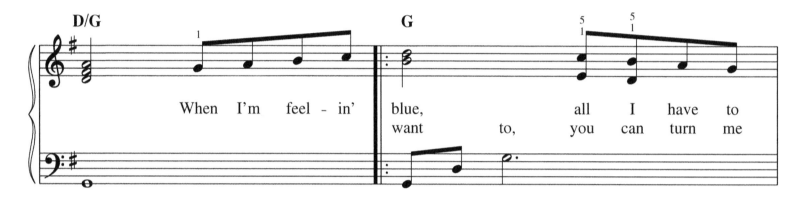

When I'm feel - in' blue, all I have to
want to, you can turn me

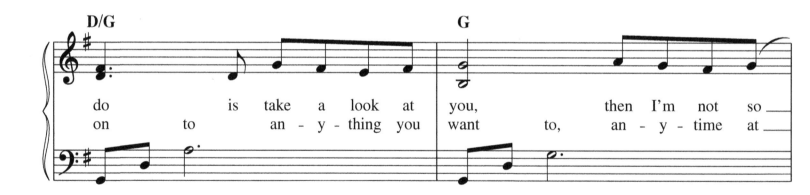

do is take a look at you, then I'm not so
on to an - y - thing you want to, an - y - time at

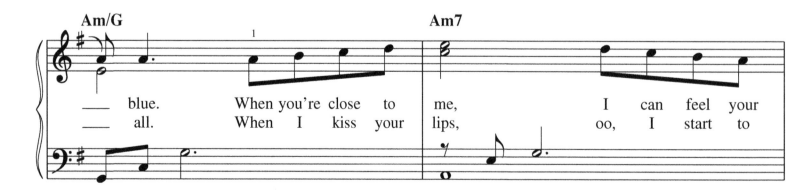

___ blue. When you're close to me, I can feel your
___ all. When I kiss your lips, oo, I start to

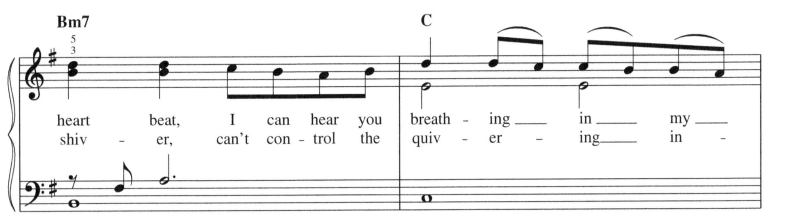

heart beat, I can hear you breath - ing ___ in ___ my ___
shiv - er, can't con - trol the quiv - er - ing ___ in -

ear. Would - n't you a - gree, ba - by, you and
side. Would - n't you a - gree, ba - by, you and

1.

me got a groo-vy kind of love. An - y-time you
me got a groo-vy kind of

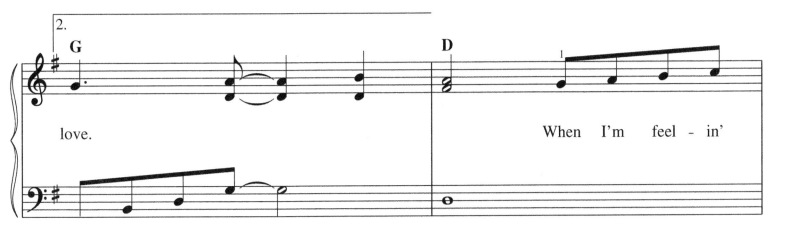

2.

love. When I'm feel - in'

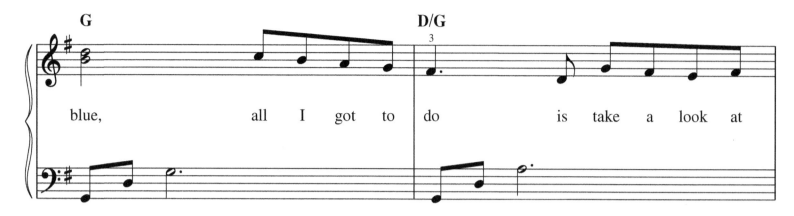

blue,   all I got to do   is take a look at

you,   then I'm not so ___ blue.   When you're in my

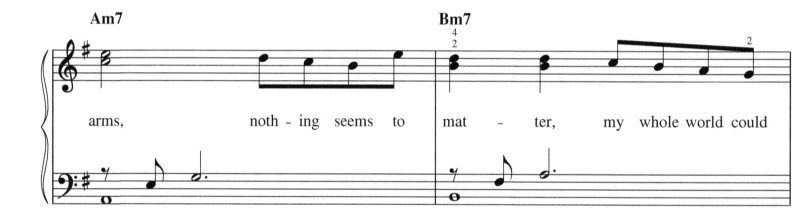

arms,   noth - ing seems to mat - ter,   my whole world could

shat - ter, I don't ___ care.___   Would - n't you a -

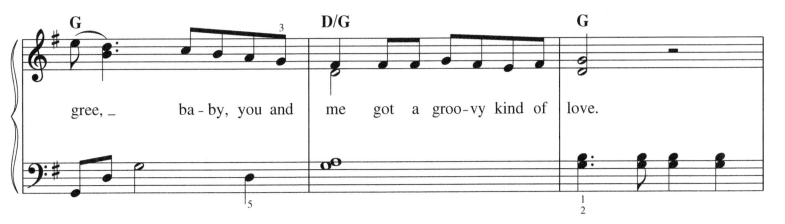

gree, _ ba - by, you and me got a groo-vy kind of love.

We got a groo-vy kind of love. We got a groo-vy kind of

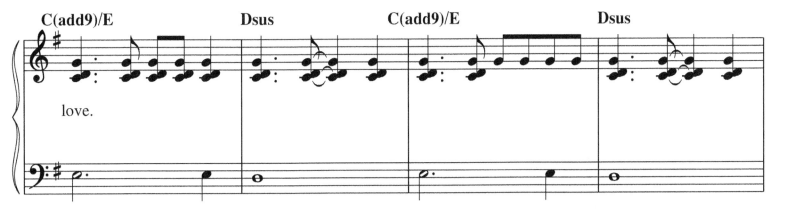

love.

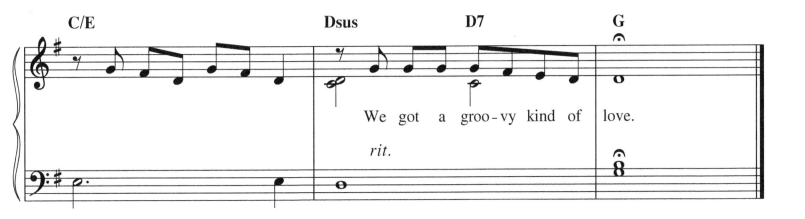

We got a groo-vy kind of love.

rit.

IN THE AIR TONIGHT

Words and Music by
PHIL COLLINS

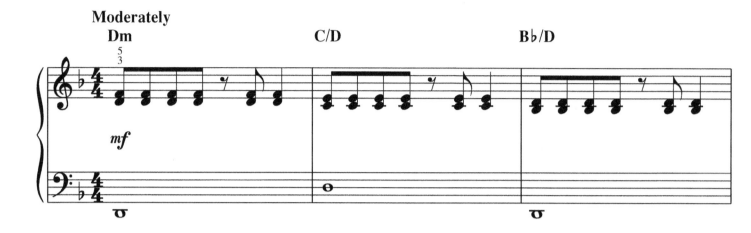

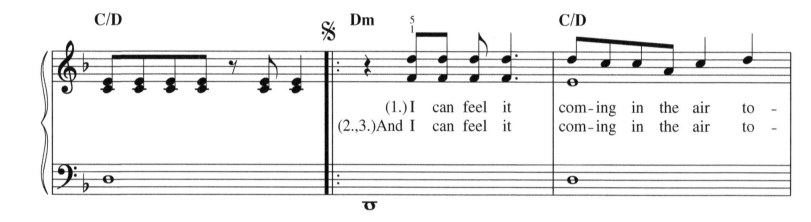

(1.)I can feel it com-ing in the air to -
(2.,3.)And I can feel it com-ing in the air to -

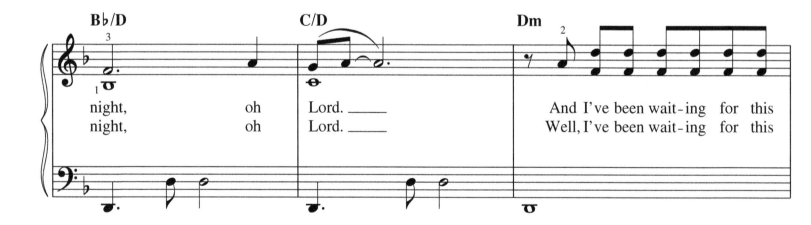

night, oh Lord. ____ And I've been wait-ing for this
night, oh Lord. ____ Well, I've been wait-ing for this

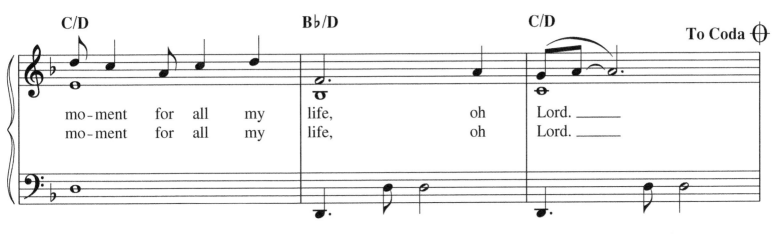

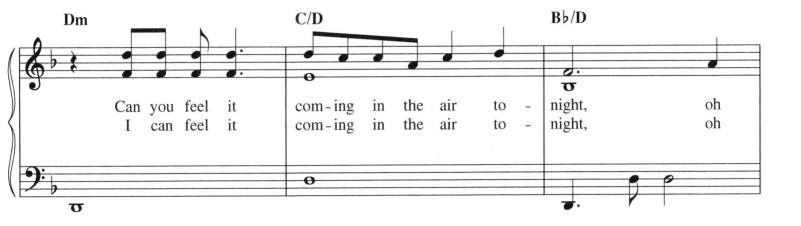

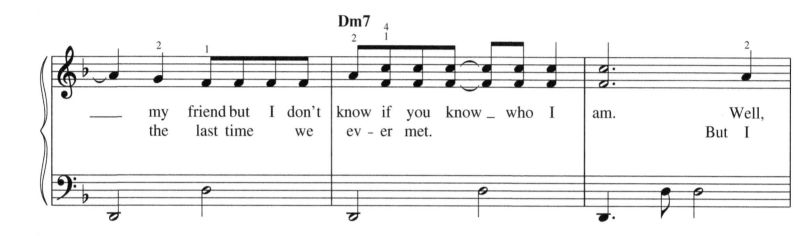

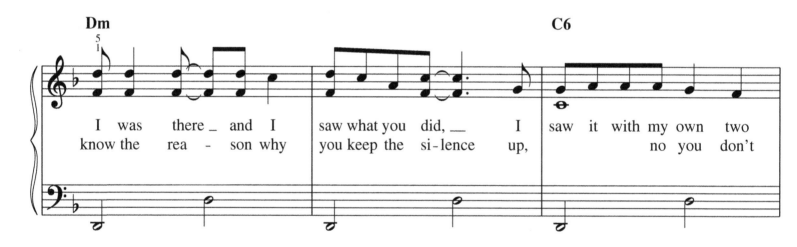

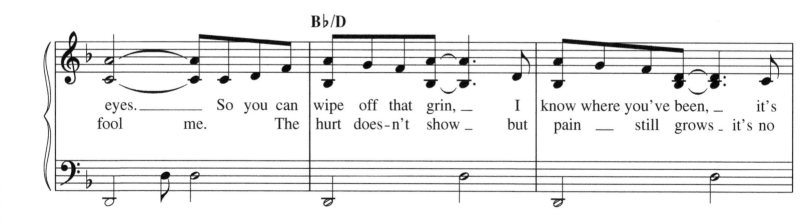

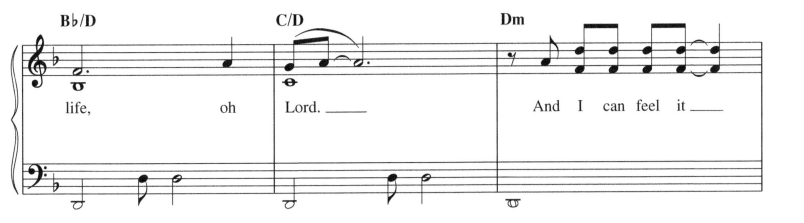

com-ing in the air to - night,   oh   Lord, _____

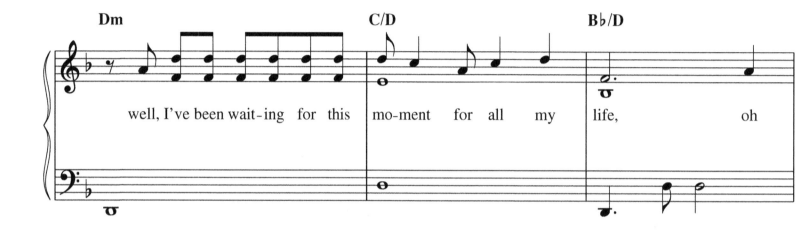

well, I've been wait-ing for this mo-ment for all my   life,   oh

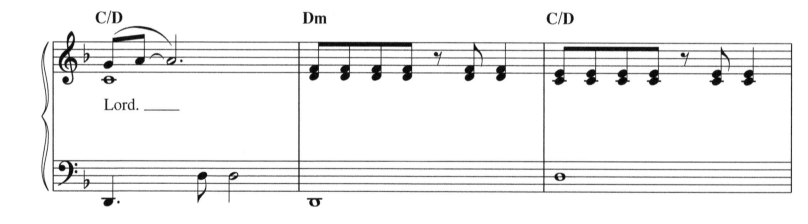

Lord. _____

rit.

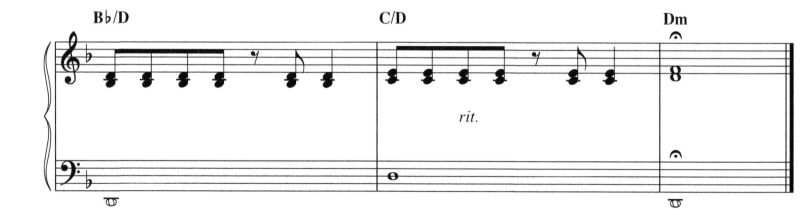

TAKE ME HOME

Words and Music by
PHIL COLLINS

Medium slow Rock Ballad

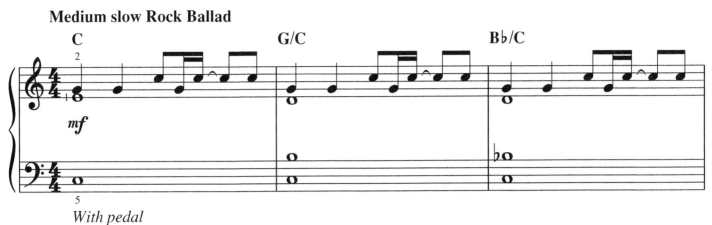

With pedal

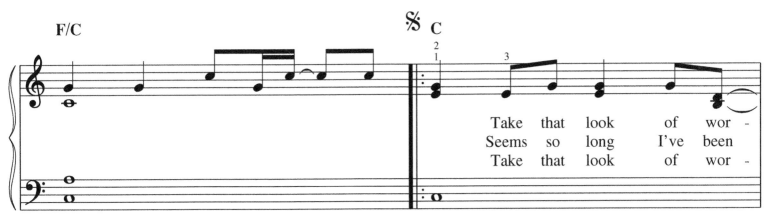

Take that look of wor -
Seems so long I've been
Take that look of wor -

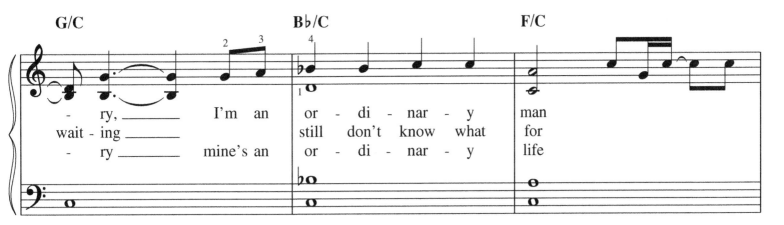

- ry, _____ I'm an or - di - nar - y man
wait - ing _____ still don't know what for
- ry _____ mine's an or - di - nar - y life

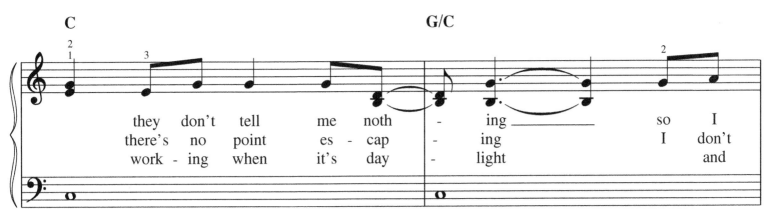

they don't tell me noth - ing _____ so I
there's no point es - cap - ing I don't
work - ing when it's day - light and

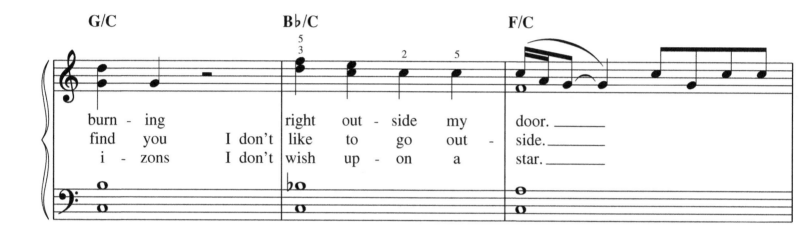

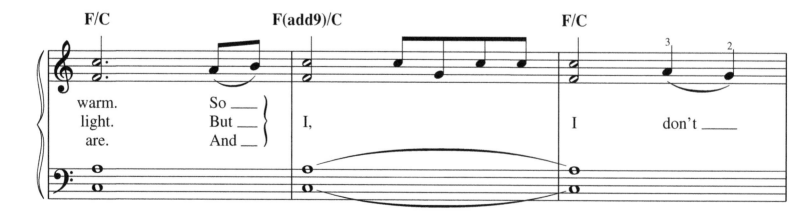

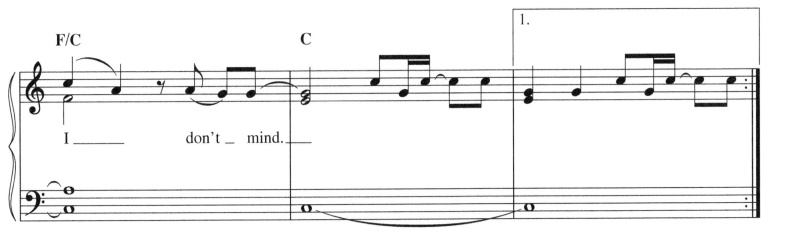

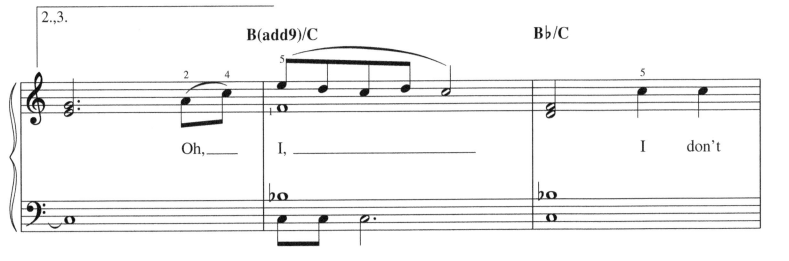

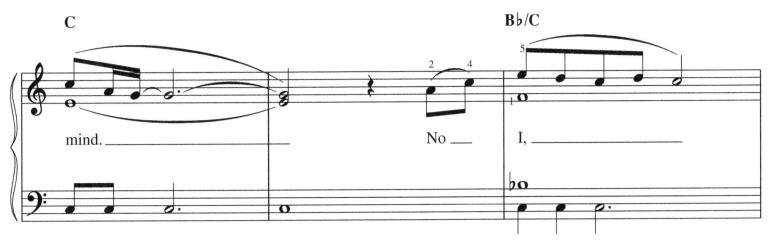

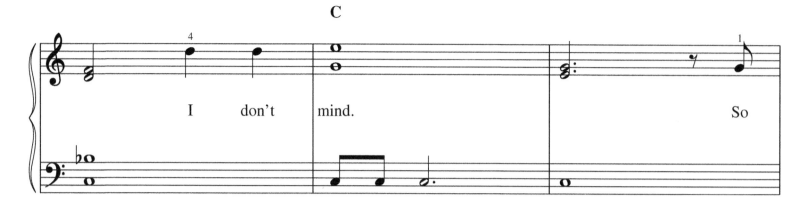

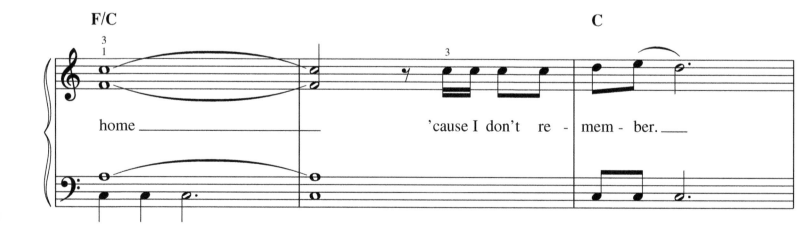

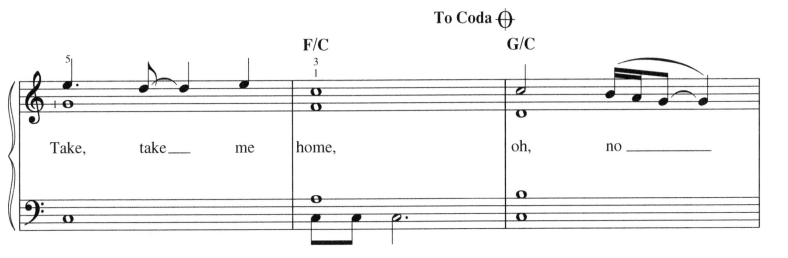

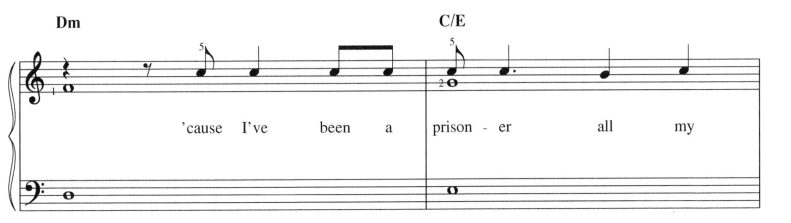

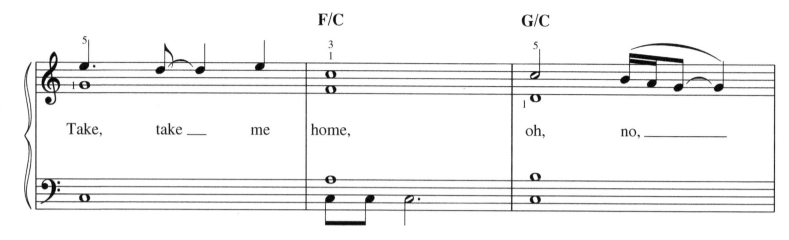

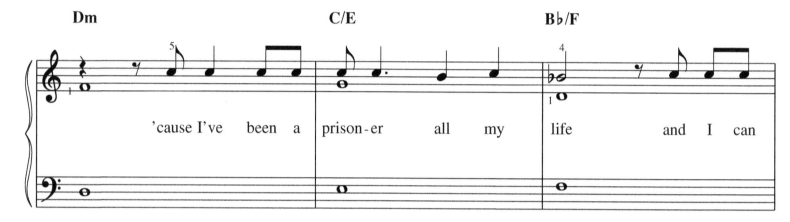